ADVENTIST CHRISTIAN SCHOOL

The Zapped Tadpole

AND MORE ANIMAL STORIES

AND
MORE ANIMAL STORIES

SANDY CHESNEY

Pacific Press Publishing Association
Boise, Idaho
Oshawa, Ontario, Canada

Edited by Bonnie Widicker
Designed by Tim Larson
Cover and illustrations by Kim Justinen
Typeset in 11/13 Century Schoolbook

Copyright © 1991 by
Pacific Press Publishing Association
Printed in United States of America
All Rights Reserved

Library of Congress Cataloging-in-Publication Data:
Chesney, Sandy.
   The zapped tadpole and more animal stories / Sandy Chesney.
      p.   cm.
   Summary: A collection of animal stories with a Christian theme.
   ISBN 0-8163-1029-7
   1. Animals—Religious aspects—Christianity—Juvenile literature. 2. Children—Religious life. 3. Christian life—1960- —Juvenile literature. [1. Animals. 2. Christian life.] I. Title.
BT746.C44 1991   90-21130
242'.62—dc20   CIP
                                                    AC

Dedication

To my encouraging mother

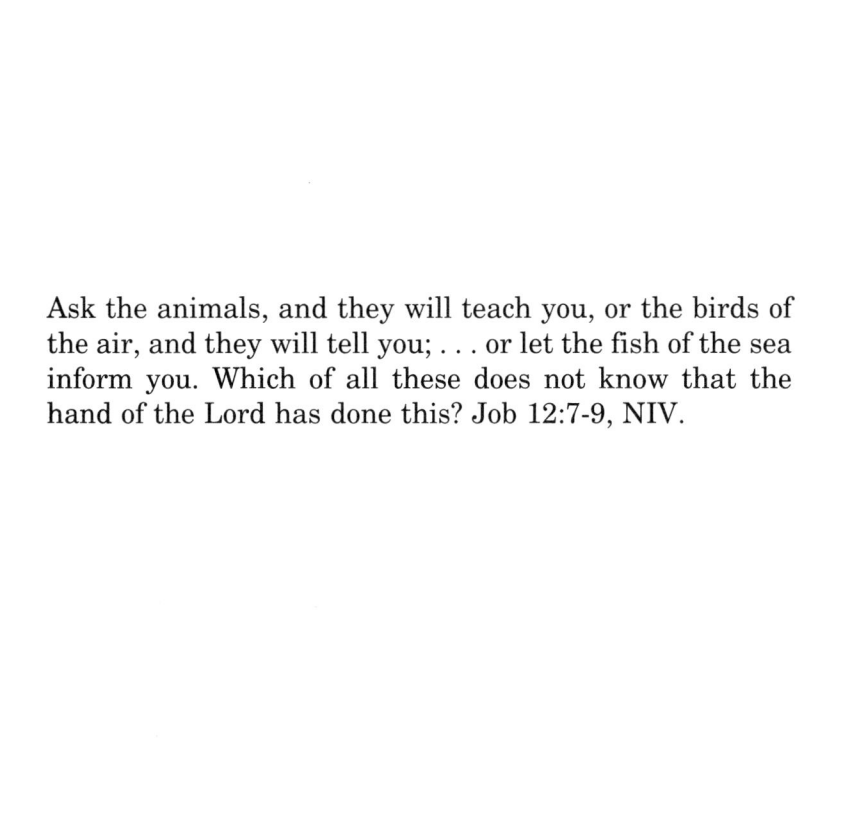

Ask the animals, and they will teach you, or the birds of the air, and they will tell you; . . . or let the fish of the sea inform you. Which of all these does not know that the hand of the Lord has done this? Job 12:7-9, NIV.

Contents

Chapter	1.	The Zapped Tadpole	11
Chapter	2.	"Hold on Tight!"	14
Chapter	3.	Markie Paints the Carpet	19
Chapter	4.	Markie Runs Away	22
Chapter	5.	The Abandoned Fawn	29
Chapter	6.	Bear Wisdom	33
Chapter	7.	The Kind Bison	37
Chapter	8.	Danger in the Henhouse	42
Chapter	9.	A Cat That Takes Showers	47
Chapter	10.	The Grateful Mountain Goats	50
Chapter	11.	Patches Saves Jimmy	55
Chapter	12.	Animals Get Spankings Too	59
Chapter	13.	The Slimy Surprise	63
Chapter	14.	Selena Sunshine Madcat's Babies	67
Chapter	15.	Galileo and Griselda	71
Chapter	16.	Cisco Gets Hurt	74
Chapter	17.	Little Bit and Pest	79
Chapter	18.	A Man for a Mother	82
Chapter	19.	Lazarus the Falcon	87
Chapter	20.	Withou	91

1

The Zapped Tadpole

Rob felt as excited as a kid on the last day of school. A special pet waited for him at his home—a tadpole!

A friend had given him the tadpole for his birthday. He had to order it, and then it would be mailed to him. Rob had waited for the weather to cool before he sent for it. Mom said it would cook in the mailbox if he didn't.

Then he had to wait for it to come. Waiting seemed to take forever. But one day his mom had called him on the phone while he was playing at his friends' house. She had good news. His tadpole had arrived!

"Rob," she said. "Your tadpole came today. Do you want me to put it into its tank, or do you want to put it in when you get home?" She watched the little creature swim in its plastic bag as she talked.

"No, don't wait for me," Rob answered. "Go ahead. I don't want to take any chances with it."

"OK," Mom said. "You can see it when you get home."

But Mom ran into trouble. She cut open the bag and started to pour the tadpole and water into the tank. The water flowed out, but the tadpole stuck inside the bag. She tilted the bag up to drop the tadpole into the water. Suddenly, the tadpole gave a mighty flop and landed, not in the water, but on Rob's dresser!

THE ZAPPED TADPOLE

"Oh, no!" Mom exclaimed, trying to think of what to do. She remembered that the instructions on caring for the tadpole said *never* to touch it and *always* to keep it in the water. And here it wiggled on the dresser top!

Knowing it would die if the tadpole squirmed there for long, she tried to pick it up. But her fingers slid over its slippery skin. She ran downstairs to the kitchen. Huffing and puffing, she raced back up, carrying a spatula. (A spatula is a tool that you use to turn pancakes and eggs.)

Rushing into Rob's room, she scooped up the tadpole with the spatula and lowered it into the water. The creature sank to the bottom and lay there, gasping.

Mom stared at it. Moaning, she thought, "Rob hasn't even seen his pet yet, and I have probably killed it! What with falling six inches to the dresser, my touching it, and being out of water for a minute or two, it doesn't have a chance!"

Not knowing what else to do, she prayed. "Dear Father, You see this little tadpole. I know You made it, and You don't like to see it suffer. And my son is thrilled to have it as a pet and wants to watch it change into a frog. I think You enjoy our learning about Your creatures. So, please, God, heal it and make it strong again. Thank You. In Jesus' name. Amen."

Having turned the tadpole over to Jesus, Mom tried not to worry. She unloaded the dishwasher and swept the kitchen floor, checking on the pet every few minutes.

It was still alive when Rob got home. He bounced through the front door. "Where's my tadpole?" he asked with a happy smile.

"It's in your room," answered Mom. She caught his arm as he sped past her. "But before you go, I need to tell you about it."

THE ZAPPED TADPOLE

When Mom explained what had happened, Rob's face fell. He ran up the stairs two at a time. Mom followed. Peering into the tank, he grumbled, "It's going to die."

Mom replied, "I wouldn't be so sure, Rob. I prayed for it to live. Let's pray some more."

So they closed their eyes and again asked Jesus to help and strengthen the tadpole.

When Rob climbed into bed that night, the animal swam with its head down and its tail up. As Mom tucked Rob in, she said to herself, "The poor little thing looks like it isn't going to make it."

Wondering if there was anything more that she could do, she got the instructions book from the closet shelf. Thumbing through the book, she found a surprise.

"Listen to this!" she said. She read aloud, "When your tadpole is swimming head down—tail up, it is happy and adjusted to its new home."

"Great!" yelled Rob. He and mom grinned at each other.

The next morning, the tadpole swam contentedly all over the tank. Rob and his mom thanked God for taking care of it. And there is more to this story.

Usually it takes three to four weeks for a tadpole to change into a frog, but Rob's very strong tadpole changed completely in only ten days! Rob decided that God must have zapped it with a little of His God-power! All because He cared about a young boy and a very small tadpole.

2

"Hold on Tight!"

Her braids bouncing, five-year-old Tiffany skipped ahead of her older brother and sister, Michael and Jennifer. Her family, on vacation in the Black Hills of South Dakota, was going horseback riding. Tiffany adored horses. She felt so excited; there was no way she could keep still!

After entering the corral, Mom and Dad filled out papers while the kids checked out the horses. Several bays, an appaloosa mare, and a chestnut pony stood calmly munching their feed. Their mouths rolled from side to side as they chewed.

Tiffany ran to the pony immediately.

"Can I ride you today?" she asked him as she reached out to stroke the white blaze on his face. Saying hello, the pony twitched his ears.

A slight frown on her face, Mom walked over to Tiffany. "The wranglers who take care of the horses choose which horse everyone will ride. But don't you want to ride with your dad?" she asked. She raised her eyebrows at Dad. "What do you think?"

Seeing Mom's concern, Dad said, "I think she'll be safe enough. The horses just walk following each other on this trail ride."

A man carrying a heavy saddle came out of the barn.

"HOLD ON TIGHT!"

"She can ride the pony. We'll tie a lead rope from her pony to the horse in front," he said as he struggled with the awkward load.

Mom smiled at Tiffany. "I guess it's OK. Will you hold on tight?"

"Oh, yes. Oh, boy!" exclaimed Tiffany. "What's the pony's name?"

"Wildfire," replied the man.

"Hi, Wildfire. I'm Tiffany," the little girl said.

Soon the whole family rode tall and happy on the horses. The lead wrangler led the way through the gate and into the hills. Tiffany clutched the saddle horn—the pointed part in front of her. Because she was so short, her feet stuck out like two extra humps on the saddle. The stirrups dangled far below.

As she got used to the rolling rock of the horse's walk, she looked around. A man on the appaloosa led the way, with the lead rope swinging between his horse and Tiffany's. Michael rode the horse just behind her. Jennifer followed him on a pretty bay, while Mom and Dad brought up the rear.

Another ranch hand trotted alongside, making sure the ride went smoothly. His horse's hooves bit into the dust, sending up little puffs like smoke. He kept reminding Michael's horse to keep up with the others.

"Zoomie! Catch up!" he said.

Zoomie obediently broke into a trot and caught up. But soon he slowed into his usual easygoing walk and fell behind again.

"Some Zoomie you are!" grumbled Michael.

Wildfire, on the other hand, needed no encouragement to keep up. He stayed right behind the lead horse and trotted every time he could. Leaning over to pat him on the neck, Tiffany grinned so big her face hurt.

15

THE ZAPPED TADPOLE

Tiffany thought riding was terrific fun! A cool breeze swept across the hills. Evergreen trees, rocks, and wildflowers in cheery colors dotted the rolling land. Overhead, the sun shone brightly, warming Tiffany's cheeks. She beamed with joy.

Tiffany might not have smiled if she had known that the lead rope between the front horse and Wildfire bothered the front horse. Swinging and slapping, the rope smacked the horse on the rear. This annoyed her, and she snorted with disgust. When the rope suddenly slipped and rubbed under her tail, she gave a startled whinny!

Hurting and scared, the front horse tried to get away from the rope. She bucked and ran up the hillside. And, since Tiffany's pony Wildfire was tied to her, she took Wildfire with her. "Whoa, girl!" yelled the man riding the horse.

Hearing the commotion, Mom glanced up to see Tiffany's frightened pony jump and kick. Then Wildfire galloped away too. The second ranch hand charged after the terrified animals, shouting, "Whoa!"

"Tiffany, hold on!" Mom and Dad yelled at the same time. "Hold on!" Catching a quick look at Tiffany's face, they saw a determined little girl. Her mouth was set in a straight line; her eyebrows knitted together in concentration. Her knuckles turned white from hanging on so tightly. She was not going to let this pony throw her!

The wrangler in front pulled on the appaloosa's reins, shouting, "Whoa, girl! Calm down!" The other man grabbed Wildfire's reins. They soon quieted the horses with soothing words and touches. "Are you OK?" the men asked Tiffany. Mom and Dad watched, still holding their breath.

"I'm fine," Tiffany said. "Did I do OK?" She wiped

"HOLD ON TIGHT!"

sweat off her forehead with the back of her hand.

One man laughed. "You'll be ready for the rodeo before we know it!"

Tiffany waved at her parents as the men brought the horses back to the trail. Mom and Dad blew out their breath with relief. Soon the group formed a line again and finished their ride.

Sometimes our lives can be going smoothly like it was for Tiffany. Then, all of a sudden, Satan throws in problems to frighten us, and he tries to make us fall away from Jesus. When that happens, we need to do what Tiffany did. We need to hang on to Jesus with all our strength, so *we* won't fall off, either. He will help us hold on to Him. Isn't He super?

3
Markie Paints the Carpet

Markie is a funny Persian cat that knows how to get into trouble!

One day in the summertime, Daddy painted the walls of the house that he, Mommy, baby Jessica, and Markie lived in. Using a roller and a roller pan, he stroked up and down, up and down the wall. He watched carefully as he smoothed the cream-colored paint over the yellow underneath.

Daddy concentrated so hard on his work that he didn't notice Markie taking his afternoon stroll down the hall. Markie spotted the roller pan almost full of paint. He eyed it curiously. He seemed to think, "I wonder what that stuff is?"

Now Markie knew that paper felt nicely crunchy to lie on, and metal felt even better, for its coolness soaked through his thick fur.

This pan looked like metal. Markie licked his right shoulder and thought this over. The pan was about the right size for him to curl up in. The edges curved up. He could snuggle and rest against them. Maybe he could prop his head on the edge and rub his neck against the rim. Everyone knows how much cats like their necks rubbed.

Just as Daddy looked down, Markie hopped into the

THE ZAPPED TADPOLE

paint pan! And did he get a surprise! It was wet! Do cats like to get wet? No! So what do you think Markie did? You are right. He jumped right back out of the pan and ran as fast as his short little legs would go, spreading cream-colored kitty prints across the chocolate-brown carpet!

Daddy yelled and lunged for Markie, but Markie flew between his hands. Daddy dropped his roller brush and ran after poor Markie, who was now so scared he ran as if a snarling dog were chasing him. Down the hall, through the living room, across the kitchen, and into the family room Markie raced, leaving a trail of cream pawprints. Daddy followed, yelling, "Stop, Markie, stop!" Do you think Markie stopped? No, he kept right on running.

Changing baby Jessica's diaper on her bed, Mommy heard the noise. She quickly fastened the diaper and left Jessica on the bed. She dashed through the hall to find out what was wrong. "Oh, no!" she moaned when she saw all the Markie steps outlined in paint. Following Daddy's bellows, she tore into the family room.

Daddy went one way. Mommy went the other, and Markie found himself cornered. He gave a sad meow as Daddy scooped him up. Mommy fetched a wet washcloth from the kitchen and started wiping his paws. But it soon became clear that this wouldn't do a good enough cleaning job. So Mommy and Daddy carried Markie to the kitchen sink to do a thorough job of scrubbing his feet.

Markie meowed in misery at the sight of all that water. But he had to put up with all the dipping and washing. Mommy soon dried his dripping paws, petted him reassuringly, and put him into the laundry room to keep him out of the paint while the cleanup began.

MARKIE PAINTS THE CARPET

Daddy started scouring the kitchen Markie prints when Mommy suddenly remembered baby Jessica. She hurried into the bedroom only to find no Jessica!

Jessica had recently learned how to get down from the bed. When Mommy left, Jessica had backed her baby legs off the side of the bed to the floor. She crawled down the hall to see what she could find. And guess what she found? There lay the roller pan, paint, and roller brush.

"Oh, boy!" baby Jessica might have thought. "I saw Daddy doing this. I wonder how it works."

She picked up the handle and tried to lift it up to the wall, but it was too heavy. She found that it worked just as well on the floor, and the cream color showed up better against the brown carpet. So Jessica rolled paint back and forth, back and forth. This was fun! No wonder Daddy did it all day! It colored her legs nicely too.

Mommy came around the corner to find the baby laughing and painting a three-feet square section of the floor. And painting Jessica. It was Mommy's turn to scream.

In the end, Markie, Daddy, Mommy, Jessica, and lots of carpet needed a *big* washing. What a mess!

Boys and girls, sometimes our lives go like that day. We do something that we aren't supposed to and wind up making an awful mess. We get into as much trouble as Markie did. Then Jesus helps us straighten things out. He helps us clean up if we ask Him to. And best of all, He still loves us, just as Daddy and Mommy still loved Jessica and silly old Markie.

4
Markie Runs Away

Markie was a Persian cat. On his fourteenth birthday, he made the very bad decision to run away. Little did he know the trouble he headed for!

For one thing, a fourteen-year-old cat is an old cat. Much too old to be roaming the streets. For another, Markie had lived as a house cat all his life. He had no idea how to survive in the outside world of dogs, other cats, and cars. He didn't even know how to catch a mouse or a bird for a meal!

Normally, Markie would not have dreamed of running away. He was happy with his family of a mom, dad, and three children. But his family went on vacation, leaving him in the care of another family.

Oh, the other family treated him nicely enough. They learned to feed him when he sat by his bowl and looked sad. They scratched the good spot behind his ears every day. But still he wanted his owners. On his birthday, he found a wide-open door. He saw his chance to go find his people. Taking that chance, he strutted out the door.

Markie padded down the sidewalk, confident of finding his family. The bright sunshine warmed his fur. He came to a corner. He turned and trotted on. He rounded another corner.

MARKIE RUNS AWAY

But his family didn't live on that street or the next or the next. Markie kept walking. Soon his old feet began to hurt, and his tummy became empty. No affectionate family came to feed him or pet him. He began to realize that he was in trouble. "Meoowrl!" he cried, but nobody answered. Realizing that he was totally, hopelessly *lost*, he crawled under a bush, curled up, and fell into an easy sleep.

The new day went much the same. He wandered on and on, searching with no luck. A few cats warily watched him pass by, but they seemed to realize that he was harmless. He found a puddle to cool his dry throat. Toward evening, Markie thought he couldn't walk any farther without food. Sitting down, he saw a large dark-haired woman step outside her front door.

Slowly, he walked toward her. She looked nice. "Meoow?" he asked.

"Well, where did you come from?" she said as she bent over to pet him. "Are you hungry?"

"Meow!" Markie answered.

The nice lady went into her house and came out carrying a bowl of milk. "I don't have any cat food, but maybe you'll like this," she said. Markie lapped the milk so fast that he couldn't answer.

After he finished dinner, Markie sat on his haunches and cleaned his face. This lady was kind, but he wanted to find his own family. So on he went.

Markie spent the next days roaming the neighborhood without success. Once a dog growled and barked at him, scaring him until his hair stood straight up. Markie crouched, ready to fight. But the dog was closed inside a fence and couldn't reach the cat.

He found meals wherever he could. Once Markie watched from under a parked car, as another cat ate its

THE ZAPPED TADPOLE

dinner on a porch. Markie helped himself to the leftovers.

Another time, a kind man with blue-striped sneakers fed him cat food until his belly felt tight and round. Still Markie wandered on.

After ten days of searching, the cat began to wonder if he would ever see his family again. His bruised and sore paws ached with each step. Tangled with small sticks and burrs, the hair on his belly pulled painfully as he walked. He shivered, he hurt from tiredness, and his tummy felt like it was about to cave in. To top off all his problems, it began to rain. Hard. Markie felt so weary that he lay down in the middle of the street.

A car rumbled toward Markie. "Screech!" the brakes screamed as the car stopped. A man with big brown boots jumped out. "What in the—" he said. "It's a cat! What are you doing here? Come here, kitty!"

As the booted man came up, terrified Markie scurried under some scruffy bushes. "I never saw a cat lie in the road before," the man said as he climbed back into his car. Markie's heart beat fast as he watched the car pull away.

By this time, Markie's hope was just about gone. He dragged himself through the rain to the nearest house. Here he discovered a porch to hide under for shelter. He crawled in and tried to lick himself dry. Curling up, he shook until he fell asleep.

The following morning, the owners of the house discovered Markie under their porch. "Come on out, kitty," they coaxed. But the cat felt so upset, afraid, and worn out that he didn't move. The owners finally set a bowl of fresh cat food on their front porch and left.

The smell of the food drifted down to the kitty. In a little while he pulled himself out. Up the steps he plodded. Finding the food, he gulped it down greedily.

MARKIE RUNS AWAY

Looking around, he saw a plastic cat house beside the bowl. A soft rug lay inside. His tummy full, Markie crept in and slept again.

When he awakened to find the bowl full again, he decided to stay at this house. He had almost given up hope of finding his family. At least here he had food, shelter, and rest. So there he stayed.

Seventeen days after Markie ran away, his owners returned from vacation to learn that he was missing. The kind people who had been taking care of him had called and searched diligently for him. They even passed out flyers offering a reward for getting him back—with no luck.

"We're so sorry," they said to Markie's family. "We looked and looked." The mom who owned Markie started to cry.

"He's so *old!*" she sobbed. "How could he survive for seventeen days?" Dad put his arms around her as she dampened his shirt with her tears.

After a few minutes, Mom yanked out a tissue, wiped her nose, and announced, "I'm not giving up on Markie yet. I'm going to look for him!" Putting on a raincoat, she moved toward the door.

"We want to go too!" the children shouted.

Dad pulled his raincoat from the closet and announced, "We'll all go."

Soon they wandered through the neighborhood, shouting, "Markie! Mar-kie! Kitty, kitty, kitty!" The smallest child said, "Markie. We care about you!" But no answering meow came that night.

While Dad worked the next day, Mom typed papers to pass out. The papers said:

LOST near Malcolm Street

Fourteen-year-old Persian cat. Tan with orange eyes.

25

THE ZAPPED TADPOLE

Children's pet—needs special food. If found, please call 442-3721. $50 reward.

The children unfastened a picture of Markie from an old photo album. Armed with the reward notices and the picture, the family returned to the streets.

"Have you seen this cat?" they asked.

"No. Sorry," people said.

After a while, they went up to the large dark-haired lady's door. "Have you seen our kitty?" the children inquired.

"Why—yes, I recognize him from the picture," the lady answered. "It was about two weeks ago. I gave him some milk."

The children jumped up and down. "Where is he now?"

"I haven't seen him since then. I'm sorry," responded the lady when she saw their faces turn sad. "But I'll call you if I do."

"Thank you," said the children, and on they went.

A few houses and a few no's later, another person reported spotting Markie. But it had been more than a week ago there too.

The children began to tire. "Let's go home," they said. "We're hungry."

"Let's try two more houses," Mom encouraged. "We'll go home after that and look for Markie again tomorrow."

"OK," said the kids.

Two houses later, a curly-haired man wearing cowboy boots opened the door.

"We've lost our cat," Mom said, holding up the picture. "Have you seen him?"

The man squinted through the screen door. "Wait a minute. Let me look at that picture." He opened the door wider.

MARKIE RUNS AWAY

"Yes. I saw this cat. He was lying in the street, oh, maybe four nights ago."

Mom swallowed to get up her courage. "Was he—was he dead?"

"Oh, no," the man answered. "I stopped my car to find out what was wrong with him. When I came close, he ran up Mayflower Street." The man pointed. "You might check up that way."

"Thank you!" Mom said. "We'll do that!"

Their energy and spirits renewed, the family quickly ran up the street where the man had pointed. Mayflower Street began with a vacant overgrown lot. Just past the lot sat a green house.

Mom and the kids tramped up the steps to the front door. Mom rang the doorbell and glanced down. And there lay Markie inside the cat house!

With his paws crossed, he calmly watched his beloved family, who had finally come for him!

Mom gathered Markie into her arms. The children crowded close, petting and exclaiming over him. Markie blinked, and purred and purred and purred.

We may be like Markie, waiting for Jesus to come and take us home. We know that He loves us and will come for us, just like Markie knew this about his family. We also might be tired, discouraged, and ready to give up—maybe even hungry! But we must patiently wait and not give up, because our Father *will come* for us too!

27

5

The Abandoned Fawn

On a sunny spring morning, Mr. Bell stepped out onto his front step carrying his camera. With only three shots left on the roll of film, he looked for something to take pictures of.

Deciding to photograph his house, he walked into the yard. As he raised the camera to his eyes, he saw a small movement underneath the porch. He crept over for a better look. When he realized what was under there, he trembled with excitement.

Running on tiptoe around the corner of the house, he knocked on the open kitchen window. "Marcia, Marcia! Come out here, quick! But be quiet!" he whispered breathlessly.

Mrs. Bell didn't know what had gotten into her usually calm husband. She turned off the stove and hurried to the front door. "What's the matter, Tom?" she began. Mr. Bell cut her short with a wave of his hand.

"Come here, you've got to see this."

Mrs. Bell went over to him. "What is it?" she said. Peering into the dim light under the porch, she gasped at what she saw. For there lay a mother deer and two newborn fawns, still wet from their birth.

Mr. Bell snapped one picture after another. The mother deer eyed him warily. The fawns were so new

THE ZAPPED TADPOLE

that they could not stand yet. The mother licked them with short, rapid strokes of her tongue. Mr. and Mrs. Bell watched in fascination.

"Oh," breathed Mrs. Bell, "aren't they beautiful!"

"Gorgeous," agreed Mr. Bell.

Before long the fawns struggled to stand. They wobbled a little, but soon stood by their mother, nudging against her for food. She turned to let them nurse. After feeding, they lay back down again.

Mr. Bell was out of film.

"I think I'll drive to the store for more film," whispered Mr. Bell. His car was parked in the driveway, about thirty feet from the deer family. Mr. and Mrs. Bell had been very careful not to get too close to the little family. But when Mr. Bell started the car, the noise startled the mother deer.

Away she bolted, across the grassy fields that bordered the Bells' home, toward the mountains. Mrs. Bell's mouth fell open. "Oh, no," she moaned.

The fawns watched their mama leave. The largest struggled to its feet and tottered off after her. The little one also stood up. It took a couple of timid steps. But it was just too weak and too new to follow and slumped to the ground.

Mr. Bell, dismayed, swung his legs out of his car. "I didn't know that would happen," he said. He and his wife looked at the remaining fawn.

"What are we going to do with it?" she asked.

"If we leave it alone, I think the mother will be back," he answered.

But several hours passed, and she didn't come back. The Bells stayed inside the house, hoping that she would return if they were out of sight. They checked on the fawn after a few hours. It was beginning to show signs of

THE ABANDONED FAWN

being hungry and weak. Still no Mama came.

By late afternoon, the baby deer could no longer stand. By the time darkness fell, it couldn't raise its head. It began to breathe in an uneven rhythm. Growing more and more concerned, Mr. and Mrs. Bell had to decide what to do.

"If we feed it, it may smell like people, and the mother may never come," Mr. Bell stated.

"But if we don't feed it, it's going to die!" Mrs. Bell replied.

"Let's feed it!" both of them said at the same time.

The decision made, Mr. Bell went to the store for a baby bottle while Mrs. Bell heated some milk. They quickly filled the bottle and took it out to the little animal.

Mrs. Bell scooted close, took its head in her lap, and tried to feed it. It resisted, weakly pulling its head away. Patiently she placed the nipple in its mouth again and again. No luck. Mr. Bell suddenly had an idea.

"That nipple doesn't go into its mouth very far," he observed. "I have an idea."

Hurrying into the kitchen, he found a rubber glove. Carefully holding the top of the glove, he poured it full of milk from the kettle on the stove. Then he tied the top with a rubber band, went back outside, and poked a hole in the end of one finger.

"I think this will fit the fawn's mouth better," he said.

He pried the fawn's mouth open a little while Mrs. Bell put the nipple in. It did seem to fit better, but the deer did nothing. Mr. Bell began to pump a bit on the fawn's jaws to squeeze some milk into its mouth. When the tasty warm milk trickled across its tongue, the fawn caught on and started to suck eagerly.

"Yea!" whispered Mrs. Bell. Soon the deer emptied the glove.

31

THE ZAPPED TADPOLE

Now knowing how to feed the fawn, Mr. and Mrs. Bell took turns getting up every two hours that night to feed it. For a while it didn't seem better, but neither did it get worse. They talked soothingly to it as they fed it and stroked its fur as they had seen its mother do.

By morning, the fawn could stand again. Very tired, the Bells went into the house for some breakfast. Standing by the kitchen window, Mrs. Bell called her husband.

"Look!" she exclaimed. "Look who's coming!"

Mr. Bell rushed over to the window. "It's the mother and the other baby."

They watched, hardly daring to breathe, as the two slowly came closer and closer to the house. The mother would take a few steps, then stop and listen. She seemed to want to come, but she seemed afraid too. Finally, they disappeared around the corner of the house.

Mrs. Bell wanted to peek out of the front window, where they could see the other fawn. But Mr. Bell cautioned her. "I scared her before. We had better not do anything that might startle her again."

"You're right," agreed his wife.

They waited by the kitchen window for what seemed like a long time. "She's probably nursing it," Mrs. Bell said. "I hope our smell doesn't bother her."

In a few more minutes, the doe came back around the house. This time, two fawns followed her! Strengthened by the milk, the smaller one walked steadily behind its mother and brother. Mr. and Mrs. Bell hugged with joy, thrilled to see the family back together.

Did you know that Jesus wants our families to be like this deer family? He gave us our parents to feed us, take care of us, and return for us if we get lost or left behind.

6
Bear Wisdom

Unnnnhhh. The sound rumbled across the clearing. Straining to listen, the boy turned his ear toward the grunt.

Thirteen-year-old Ryan Steele, hiking in Yellowstone Park, knew that those sounds were probably a bear grunting. But whether they came from a black bear or the more dangerous grizzly, he couldn't tell. He licked his lips as he silently asked himself, "Has it picked up my scent or spotted me?"

Ryan inched forward. Quietly, he slipped behind a thick bush and peered between the branches. There it was—a monstrous black bear, fur shining in the sunlight. Ryan's mouth fell open, and he froze. Not sensing Ryan's presence, the bear sniffed the air in the opposite direction. Soon the animal lumbered out of sight.

Ryan's knees were shaking, so he sat down. Pulling his camera out of his pocket, Ryan thought, "I sure could get a nice shot of him if he would stand up again."

He glanced at his watch. "Good," he thought. "I have another hour before Mom and Dad are expecting me back." His parents had camped just over the ridge behind him. Ryan badly wanted a picture of this bear, but he didn't want to worry his parents by being late. He gulped as he realized that they *would* worry if they

THE ZAPPED TADPOLE

knew he was taking pictures of a bear. "But if I yelled, they would hear me and come running," he reasoned.

He decided to follow along a safe distance behind the bear. He stayed well hidden, for the bear had no idea that Ryan trailed behind.

The bear stretched up, standing well over six feet tall. Ryan lifted his camera to his eyes. But the bear kept moving.

"Be still!" Ryan thought. But the animal had other plans. It waddled to a large tree and ripped at a hole in the trunk. Pieces of bark flew everywhere. Swallowing, Ryan noted the size of the bear's claws.

Suddenly, the beast threw its head back and roared, turning toward the boy. Fear poured over Ryan like ice water.

The bear moved away from the boy. It climbed over a small hill and paused to lean against a bank. Then it started swinging its arms back and forth, back and forth, in front of itself. Ryan couldn't tell what the bear was doing, but he dared not creep any closer.

The animal seemed to be digging. Then it raised a muddy paw and stroked its muzzle. Intrigued, Ryan forgot about taking pictures. "What in the world is the bear doing?" he wondered.

Climbing again to the top of the hill, the beast plopped down with a loud grunt. It raised its mud-streaked nose into the crisp fall air. Ryan shivered, hoping that the bear's sniffing didn't mean that it smelled boy. No, the animal just sat with drying mud caked on its nose for about ten minutes. Then it scooted back down the hill and started digging again.

Soon it went back up the hill and lifted its snout like before. Fascinated, Ryan saw it repeat the whole process three times.

BEAR WISDOM

Finally, the bear heaved itself up and returned to the tree that it had clawed before. After a few more vicious rips, it scooped something out and licked its paws hungrily.

Wide-eyed, Ryan watched it eat.

"I can't believe this!" he said to himself. He closed his eyes for a minute, thinking about the wisdom God had given this bear. Then he trotted off to tell his parents what the bear had been doing. After being stung once, it had covered its nose with mud three times and let it dry in the autumn sunshine. In this way, the bear had protected its only tender spot in order to enjoy its favorite meal—honey!

7
The Kind Bison

After Jesus returns and sets up His kingdom, the animals will be tame and kind to each other. You will be able to play with lions, bears, and other fierce beasts, and you will never get hurt! Would you like to read about a buffalo on earth now that was gentle to another buffalo?

Ten-year-old Ben and his family headed on vacation for Wind Cave National Park in South Dakota. It was Labor Day weekend, and Ben's dad, a nature photographer, hoped to take some wildlife photos. Ben wanted mostly to explore.

"Hurrah!" Ben whooped as Dad finally parked their car at the campsite. "I'm sure glad to get out of here!" Climbing out of the back seat, he tore off in a run to stretch his legs.

"Young man, we need your help," Dad called.

"Oh, OK," Ben answered. "I'll be right there."

"Sure would like to check out those prairie dog holes," he mumbled to himself, "but I guess I'll have to wait a little longer."

After helping set up camp, Ben wandered about. The barking prairie dogs scolded him from a distance, then popped into their holes whenever he came close. Ben chuckled.

THE ZAPPED TADPOLE

Ben looked back toward the tent as a ranger truck pulled up in a cloud of dust. "I wonder why he's here," Ben said as he dashed back to camp.

Ben's dad shook hands with the ranger.

"Hello, I'm John Michaels. This is my wife Mary and my son Ben," Ben's dad said.

"Pleased to meet you," said the ranger. "I'm Jake Edwards. I just wanted to stop by and caution you. A young bull bison has been hit by a car up the road about a mile. It's mating season, and the bison are violent anyway. If this one is in pain, he may be very dangerous. Be sure to stay in your car if you go near there." He took off his sunglasses and wiped them against his pants leg.

"We will," Dad responded. "Thanks for warning us."

After the ranger left, Dad turned to Mom and Ben. "Are you two ready to take a ride and see some animals?"

"Sure," Ben agreed. Mom nodded. Mom and Dad got into the front while Ben slid into the back seat. The prairie dogs stuck their heads out of their holes to watch them drive off.

A few minutes later, Dad came across a line of cars parked along the roadside. "Must be that injured bison," he said. Ben peered through the window.

"Look, Dad!" Ben shouted. "There's a whole herd of 'em!"

Sure enough, a large number of bison stood grazing. Not seeming to care that people watched them, they formed a kind of circle.

"What are they doing?" Ben asked.

"I'm not sure. Wait! I think the one that's hurt is in the center of their circle," Dad said. "Yes, he is. You can see him a little through there." Dad pointed.

"Yeah, there he is." Ben shaded his eyes to see better.

THE KIND BISON

"He's lying down. I wonder how badly he's hurt."

"No way of knowing," Dad answered. "Do you see that large bull?" He pointed to a huge shaggy buffalo with three smaller ones near him.

"Yes."

"That's an old, strong bull. He's kind of like the king of the herd. The small bison near him are his cows. During mating season, an older bull like him will have several females that he considers his wives."

The large bull snorted loudly as if he knew that he was being talked about. Dad rolled down his window to take a few shots of the dark, hairy creatures. Soon he finished and was ready to drive on.

Later that afternoon, Ben's family returned to camp past the place where the herd had been grazing. Stopping the car, they found most of the herd gone.

"Well, I'll be!" Dad exclaimed.

Ben and Mom squinted through the window.

"The injured one is still down," Mom said. "And the others have all left—except for the one 'king' bull. Boy, that's a surprise!"

"You can say that again," Dad agreed. "Usually those two would be fighting over the females. But the big one is standing over the younger, hurt one—as if he's protecting him!"

"Do you think the big one knows that the other one is hurt?" Ben asked.

"Sure looks like it to me," Dad answered.

"Wow," Ben said, watching the two buffalo. "Here comes a ranger!" he said. "What's he doing?"

"I don't know, Ben. We'll see." The three of them watched as the ranger walked slowly toward the two bison. "I think he's trying to find out how badly the bison is hurt," Dad said.

THE ZAPPED TADPOLE

Suddenly, the big bison snorted and shook his head at the ranger. The ranger stopped. When the buffalo started to charge him, the ranger made a quick dash for his truck!

"Did you see that?" Ben shouted.

"Yes," Mom and Dad said. Giving up the chase, the bison went back to stand beside the injured bull.

"He is protecting him!" Dad said. "That's amazing. Normally those two would be fighting."

"The large one has lost his cows too," Mom added.

"You're right, he has," Dad said. "It looks as if he has placed aside his natural instinct to stay with this younger bull."

Ben's family watched for a few more minutes. The ranger made no more attempts to check the hurt buffalo. Not eating, the old bull kept watch.

"Let's go," Dad said. "I'm getting hungry."

"Me too!" Ben knew how Dad felt.

Soon they rolled back into their campsite. After supper and cleanup, Ben said, "Do you think we could go see whether the big buffalo is still there?"

"Sure." Dad nodded.

"You two go ahead," Mom put in. "I'll get our sleeping bags ready."

This time Dad parked the car a little distance from the bison. The two still remained as before—the hurt one down and the big one standing near him. The shadows disappeared as darkness fell. Ben and Dad sat quietly. Ben could just make out the shape of the big bull's head in the moonlight.

"Look, Ben," Dad said in a low voice.

Ben's eyes widened as the bull charged at something. He caught a glimpse of a low shape running away as he asked, "What was it?"

THE KIND BISON

"I think it was a coyote," Dad answered. "The coyote must have been hoping that the hurt bison was dead so that it could have an easy meal. That big bison is amazing." Dad shook his head. "Well, shall we go back to camp?"

Ben yawned. "Yeah, I'm sleepy."

Before long, Ben snuggled into his sleeping bag and fell asleep. He dreamed of a hurt buffalo wearing a cast and a "doctor" buffalo standing over him.

The next morning, the family drove through the prairie where the bison had been. The injured buffalo and his protector were gone.

"How about that?" Dad said. "The big guy stayed with the hurt one until he could get up and leave by himself. He stuck with him until the other one got better. He reminds me of what the animals will be like after Jesus comes. They will always be kind then."

Ben grinned. "It'll be great!" he said.

8
Danger in the Henhouse

Shep, a tan-and-white male collie dog, belonged to a nine-year-old brown-haired girl named Cassie. Cassie and he were the best of friends. Almost everything that Cassie did, Shep tagged along beside her.

Cassie and Shep lived on a farm in Tennessee. With the fun and joy of farm animals also comes work, so Cassie had chores to do.

One of Cassie's chores was gathering the eggs. Every day she and Shep tiptoed into the henhouse. Cassie slipped her hand into the nests. Sometimes a hen sitting on her nest angrily pecked at Cassie. When this happened, Shep jumped into action.

He sprang up on his hind legs and barked. Loud. Then the frightened hen flew away, leaving his precious Cassie alone.

In the afternoon, Shep raced to meet Cassie when she returned from school. His tongue lolled in a big smile; he romped in circles welcoming Cassie home.

When Cassie fed the horses, Shep watched carefully, afraid to let any of them too close to his owner. Cassie laughed at Shep for protecting her. "Silly dog!" she said with love as she hugged his furry neck.

Shep and Cassie were such pals that Shep seemed to understand Cassie's every mood. If Cassie came home

DANGER IN THE HENHOUSE

from school with a headache, Shep met her with his tail wagging, but he didn't bark or jump. Cassie wondered how he knew her head hurt.

Once, Cassie felt sad because her best friend Jill had spent all recess playing with another girl. That afternoon, Cassie sat pouting. Shep lay in the grass, resting his chin on Cassie's knee. He gazed into her eyes with his soft, shiny brown ones as if to say, "Don't worry, *I'm* your friend!"

One hot summer night, Cassie didn't sleep well. She felt cross and sleepy in the morning when her mother called her down to breakfast. "OK, OK, I'm up," she muttered to herself as she yanked on her shorts and T-shirt.

When she walked into the kitchen, she found that her mom had fixed grits and fried eggs. Cassie hated grits and she liked only scrambled eggs, so she got more upset. By the time she went out to do chores, she felt so grouchy that she slammed the back door. Her bad mood didn't get better when Mom made her come back and close the door gently.

As Cassie stepped outside, Shep bounded up to say good morning. Used to a good petting, he seemed puzzled when Cassie wouldn't pet him—or even speak to him! Trying to make friends, he ran along beside her, begging for attention. She ignored him. Then he saw that she was headed for the henhouse. He had seen danger there.

As Cassie stomped up to the henhouse, Shep barked in warning. Cassie paid no attention. As she touched the door, Shep squirmed in between Cassie and the henhouse and would not move.

Cassie finally noticed Shep. "Get out of my way, Shep," she grumbled. But Shep didn't go anywhere. Cassie pushed against Shep's side with her leg. "Come on,

43

THE ZAPPED TADPOLE

you dumb dog, I have to feed these chickens. Move!" she yelled crossly.

Shep looked at her and wagged his tail hopefully. Growing angrier, Cassie pushed harder. Shep stood his ground. At last Cassie kicked Shep as hard as she could!

Shep yelped in pain, struggling to keep his feet on the ground. He was completely confused. Cassie had never kicked him before! But still he wouldn't move from the henhouse door.

Cassie burst into tears. She ran back to the farmhouse, where she almost crashed into her father, who was coming out the back door.

"Whatever's the matter, Cassie?" he asked, putting his hands on her shoulders.

"Oh, Daddy," Cassie sobbed. "Everything's rotten today! I woke up feeling awful, and now Shep won't let me into the henhouse. I don't know what's wrong with that stupid dog!"

"Now, Cassie, calm down. There must be a good reason why Shep won't let you in." Daddy pulled out a big handkerchief and wiped at Cassie's tears. "Let's go see Shep and find what the problem is, OK?"

Cassie blew her nose. "OK," she sniffed.

Daddy led the way back to the henhouse, with Cassie right behind. Shep still lay in front of the door. He thumped his tail on the ground when he saw Daddy and Cassie.

"What's wrong, boy?" Daddy patted Shep's head. Shep watched uneasily as Daddy reached for the doorknob. Shep then got up and wedged himself between Daddy and Cassie, allowing Daddy to pass but not Cassie.

"Stay back, honey," Daddy warned as he slowly pushed against the door. "Shep knows what he's doing."

The door creaked open. Cassie peeked around her

DANGER IN THE HENHOUSE

father. Everything looked normal. Then Daddy looked around the edge of the door. Quickly he jerked back, almost knocking Cassie down.

"What is it?" Cassie asked. Daddy hurried toward the barn, with Cassie racing at his heels.

"It's a big copperhead snake," he shouted over his shoulder, as he grabbed a hoe.

After killing and burying the snake, Daddy looked for Cassie. She and Shep were sitting underneath the apple tree. Her arm lay across Shep's back. Daddy opened his mouth to talk to her, but kept quiet when he heard her praying.

"Dear God," she said, "please forgive me for kicking Shep. I didn't know he was just taking care of me. I'm sorry that I was such a grouch today. Please help me to be nice. Thank You. In Jesus' name. Amen."

Daddy smiled at his daughter. Shep licked Cassie's cheek, as if to say, "You and I will always be best buddies!"

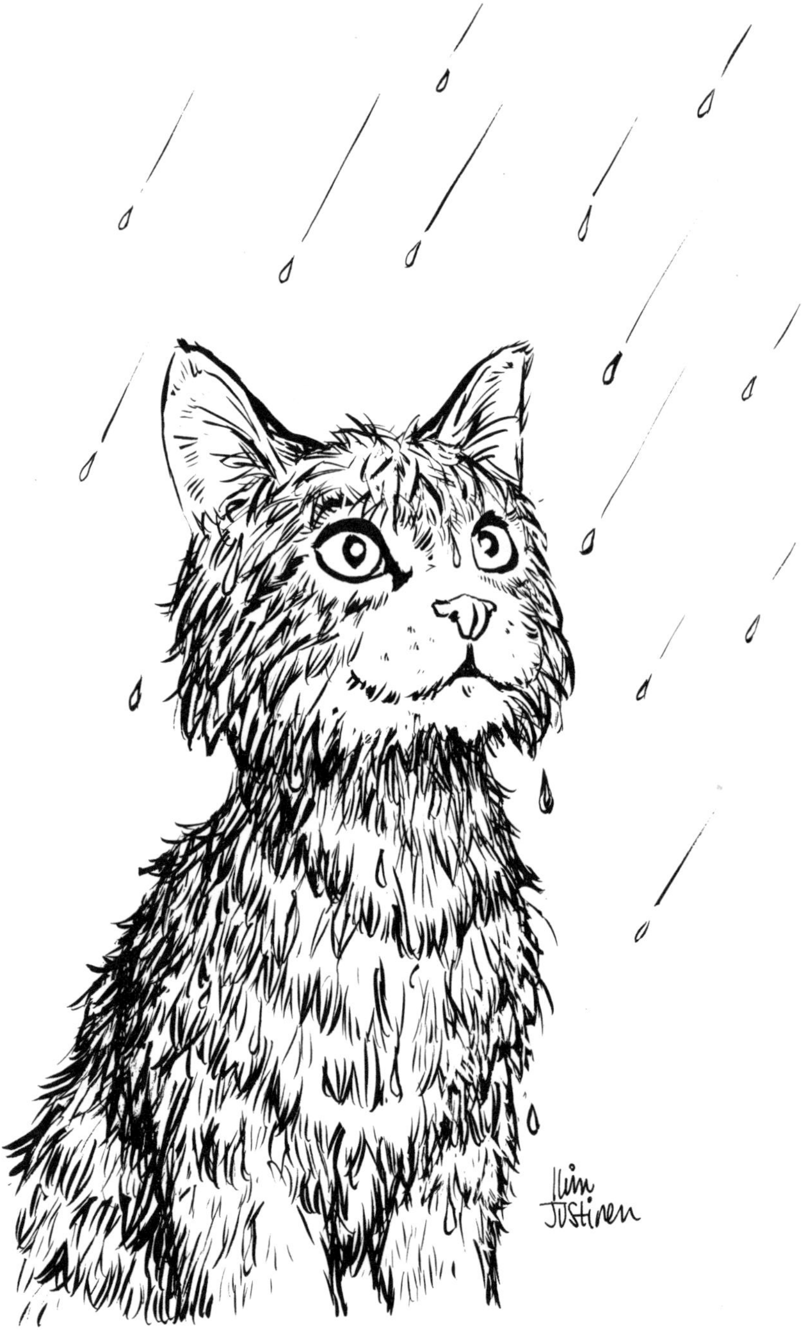

9

A Cat That Takes Showers

Jason slumped between his dad and his sister Meghan in the middle of the church pew. He wiggled and fidgeted. Wrinkling his eyebrows together, he thought about his problem. He knew he had upset Mom this morning, but what he told her was true—he didn't like to go to church!

"Wel-l-l," Jason said to himself, "I like *some* things about church. I like the kids' classes. And I think Jesus is terrific! But I can't stand sitting here! I don't even understand what's going on in the grown-up time!"

Jason's thoughts popped like a bubble as his dad nudged him.

"Do you want to go up for the children's story?" Dad whispered.

"Sure," Jason answered as he slipped past Dad and Mom. "I'll be glad to hear something fun for a change," he grumbled to himself.

Pastor Brown held the microphone and smiled at the kids. Jason scooted in beside his friend Jeremy on the front pew.

"This is a true story about a cat," Pastor Brown began, instantly catching their attention. "A young woman named Elaine lived alone in an apartment. Sometimes she felt lonely. So her parents chose an orange-and-white kit-

47

THE ZAPPED TADPOLE

ten and took her to Elaine to be company for her.

"The kitten jumped out of Elaine's mother's arms and ran up to Elaine, purring and rubbing against her legs. Elaine liked the little cat as much as it liked her. She cupped her hand under the kitten's soft furriness and picked her up. Cuddling her close to her chin, she whispered into a velvet ear, 'Aren't you a sweet girl? I'm going to call you Kneesox, because your little white feet make you look like you are wearing kneesox.' Kneesox purred her approval.

"The cat and Elaine became great pals. Everything that Elaine did, Kneesox tried also. Kneesox ate while Elaine ate and slept when Elaine slept. When Elaine bent over forward to dry her hair, she watched Kneesox behind her. So Kneesox bent way over and peered at Elaine from between her furry legs.

"Elaine had a telephone answering machine to take messages. When the phone rang, Elaine's recorded voice told the person calling that she would call them back. But when Kneesox heard her beloved Elaine talking, she jumped up on top of the machine to search for her. This often turned off the machine. Sometimes Elaine got upset at Kneesox if she missed an important call. But she wasn't angry long, because she knew that Kneesox only wanted to be close to her.

"Kneesox loved Elaine so much that she felt sad when Elaine showered in the morning. Cats normally hate water, right? Right. Although Kneesox stayed beside Elaine all the rest of the time, she sat outside the shower curtain and meowed sadly every time Elaine stepped into the shower.

" 'You silly cat!' Elaine said as she dried off. 'I'm only two feet away.' Still Kneesox cried during every shower.

"One day, the pet could stand it no longer. Hesitating

A CAT THAT TAKES SHOWERS

a little, she stretched out one paw and slipped it under the shower curtain as if to make sure Elaine was still there. She touched Elaine's foot, causing Elaine to jump.

"'Oh, Kneesox, you scared me.' Elaine peeked around the curtain. Kneesox lifted her leg and licked it dry. She blinked as if to say, 'That wasn't so bad.' After that, the cat poked her paw in the shower almost every day. Then one morning, Elaine got a big surprise.

"That morning, Elaine stepped into the shower as usual. The water streamed down her face. She felt something move beside her foot, but she was used to Kneesox's exploring. Imagine her surprise when she wiped the water from her eyes and found not just one paw in the shower but the whole kitty!

"There stood Kneesox, dripping wet! Her fur stuck together in soggy clumps. She licked at the water running down her face. She looked more like a rat than a cat! Yet Kneesox purred and meowed at Elaine as if to say, 'I love you this much!'

"Kneesox showers with Elaine every day now. The cat has let her love for her owner overcome her hatred of water. Boys and girls," Pastor Brown finished, "if there is something you don't like to do, you perhaps could let love overcome the bad feelings too. Jesus has promised that He will help us deal with any problem if we ask Him to help."

Jason swallowed hard. "Maybe I should let my love for *my* owner Jesus win over my hating to sit still in church," he thought. "Jesus has promised to help, so I can ask Him to help me like church better. Maybe He will give me some ideas of things to do during church time. I guess I need to be more like Kneesox."

And Jason found that with Jesus helping him, he had an easier time being happy in church.

49

10

The Grateful Mountain Goats

Driving up Mt. Evans, Mr. Carlisle felt as if his heart might burst with joy. A newborn baby boy slept at his home, while the endless Colorado sky beamed a brilliant blue. He planned to spend the perfect day taking pictures of mountain goats. Nature photography was both his hobby and his love. He couldn't be happier.

Humming "This Is My Father's World," he shifted gears as his truck climbed the mountain. He spotted a few goats quite a distance away but decided to continue on, hoping to find animals closer to the road. But as he drove higher, the animal life, like the trees, became sparser. So he turned around and went back to the first goats.

Parking his truck, he lifted his camera and lunch pack to his shoulders and set off after the goats. But the closer he came to them, the farther away from the road they walked. Trailing them over the snow-covered rocks was difficult. Mr. Carlisle tired quickly in the high altitude.

Brushing the snow off a big rock, he sat down to catch his breath. Then he glanced at his watch. "No wonder I don't have any energy," he said to himself. "It's way past lunchtime."

He unzipped his backpack and pulled out a sandwich,

THE GRATEFUL MOUNTAIN GOATS

then paused to thank God. "Thank You, Lord, for all the wonderful blessings You have given me. May this food make me strong so that I can work for You. In Jesus' name. Amen."

He hungrily bit into his sandwich. As he ate, he watched the goats, standing a short distance away. The goats were acting strangely. They seemed excited and upset.

Mr. Carlisle took out his binoculars for a better look. Yes, the goats *were* upset, especially one female. Over and over, she trotted to the top of an enormous boulder, pranced around frantically, then jumped down and ran to the front of the rock. This seemed abnormal to Mr. Carlisle. Something must be wrong.

His curiosity standing at attention, Mr. Carlisle shook his head a little. "What in the world is she doing?" he said to himself.

Hunger forgotten, he stuffed his half-eaten sandwich back into his pack and slowly walked toward the animals. "I'm going to find out what's going on," he said softly. "Maybe a goat is injured."

As he walked close to the goats, they scattered away from the boulder. He looked for blood on the snow or any other evidence of a hurt goat, but he found only hoof tracks.

He stood beside the huge rock wondering what was wrong with those goats. Just as he decided to finish his lunch, he heard a soft bleating sound.

Whirling about, Mr. Carlisle discovered a sharp crevice in the edge of the rock. It opened into a dark, mysterious cave. Ice and snow partially covered the opening. He cocked his head as he listened. Yes, he heard a tiny cry coming from within the cave.

His curiosity replacing his fear, he stuck his head into

51

THE ZAPPED TADPOLE

the opening of the cave. The cave was as dark as a cloudy midnight. He could see nothing. The cry sounded like a baby goat. That would explain the mother's strange behavior. He decided to go into the cave.

As he stepped into the cave, he got a big surprise. "Yiiiii!" Mr. Carlisle yelled as his feet slid out from under him and his legs flew into the air. He slid about eight feet down—into the darkness.

Rubbing his backbone where he had bounced against a rock, he sat up and peered into the darkness. As his eyes adjusted to the dim light, he could see the jagged entrance to the cave shining brighter and brighter. At the mouth of the cave, a steep wall of ice dropped to where he sat. *"That's* what caused me to fall," he thought as he straightened up.

Standing, he heard the bleating sound again—this time, much louder. Looking in the direction of the sound, he saw an eight-inch-wide crack in the floor of the cave. The cry came again—and it was a weak baa.

Mr. Carlisle looked down into the opening. Something white was wedged in the bottom. Reaching his arm into the crevice, he touched a soft, furry body. It was alive and crying. He worked his hand underneath and felt the rapid, scared heartbeat tum—tum, tum—tum against his palm. With a gentle twist, he pulled out a curly-haired baby mountain goat.

"Ooh," he breathed. He cuddled the little animal close to his chest. The baby goat didn't struggle, but lay quietly in his arms. Mr. Carlisle held and petted the fuzzy goat for a minute, realizing that somehow he had to get it out of the cave. "But how?" he wondered. The entrance was sheer ice.

Now that he could see better in the dim light, he looked around the cave. He noticed that there was no ice

THE GRATEFUL MOUNTAIN GOATS

on the right cave wall. "Maybe," he whispered to the baby goat, "just maybe, I can climb up those rocks and get us out of here."

Tucking the animal under his arm, he slowly, carefully crept up the rocks. But as he reached the mouth of the cave, his mouth fell open in surprise and fear. Not three feet from his face, mama goat stomped and pounded her hooves in the ice and snow! She wanted her baby back—now!

Both male and female mountain goats have long, pointed horns. Mr. Carlisle knew that she could use them like knives. He quickly placed the baby goat between himself and the mama, held it out, and asked, "Are you looking for your baby?"

But the rim of the cave was so icy that the baby slid right back against his chest. Even though the mother could rip him to pieces, Mr. Carlisle knew that he had no choice but to crawl out in front of her. Taking a deep breath, he did just that. He bent his knees against his chest in case the mother decided to punish him for holding her baby. With shaking hands, he placed the baby at its mother's feet.

The baby goat nestled closer to its mother. They touched noses. Mama seemed to check whether the baby was hurt. The little one started to bounce around with joy. Neither mother nor baby paid attention to Mr. Carlisle.

As the goats walked away together, Mr. Carlisle stood up. When the animals were about ten feet away from him, they stopped and turned toward the man. Both of them gave him a long look, seeming to say, "Thank you!" Then they moved away.

Mr. Carlisle says that God sent him up on the mountain that day to rescue one of His babies. I think he's right, don't you?

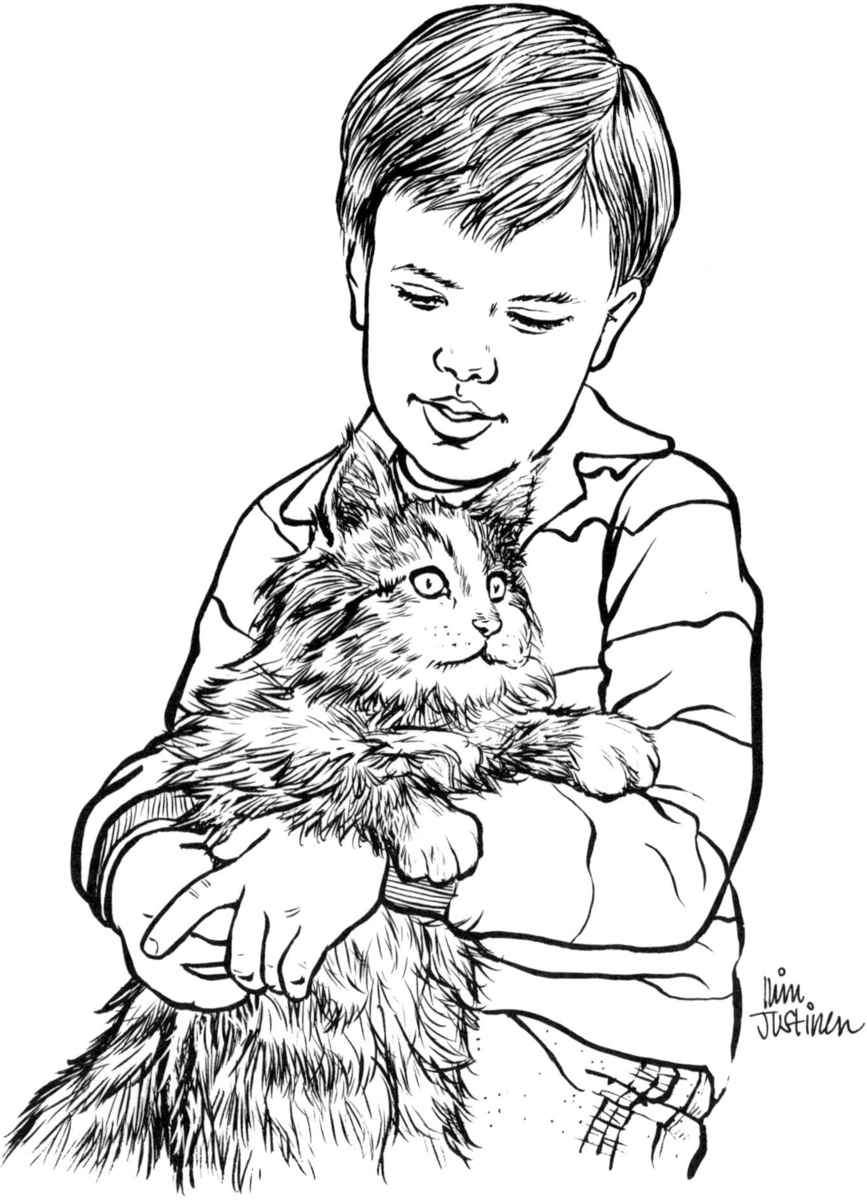
Kim Justinen

11
Patches Saves Jimmy

The Bible tells how our friend Jesus allowed people to kill Him when He lived here on earth as a man. He died for us so that we can live forever with Him. Because He loves every one of us, He gave everything He had—even His *life*—to save us. Isn't that fantastic?

You would really have to love a person *very* much before you would be willing to die for him or her, wouldn't you? Well, the Jones family has a cat that loves his boy so much that he risked his life to save him—twice!

His boy was an active four-year-old named Jimmy. Jimmy lived in the country. He had several pets, but his favorite was the black-and-white cat named Patches.

After Jimmy finished his breakfast every morning, he banged the screen door behind him as he went outside to look for Patches. Patches would watch Jimmy from behind a tree, pretending he wasn't interested in playing. But Jimmy knew how to get Patches' attention.

From his jeans pocket, Jimmy would pull out a small ball tied to a string. When Patches saw the toy, he ran up, smacking the ball with his paw. The ball bounced all around when Patches boxed. Jimmy would throw his head back and laugh happily.

Patches often rode curled up around Jimmy's neck as

THE ZAPPED TADPOLE

Jimmy played. They always played together, and they loved each other dearly.

One winter night, Jimmy slept soundly in his room. His breath whispered like tiny sighs, in and out, in and out. Patches slept in the basement, curled into a warm, furry circle. As Patches slept, the basement filled with a strange smell. The smell became stronger, until finally it woke him up. The smell was smoke.

Sensing danger, Patches leapt out of his bed and sprinted up the stairs. All was quiet, but the fire smelled stronger on the main floor of the house.

"Meeoww!" Patches wailed as he sprang into Jimmy's room. Jimmy groaned and rolled onto his side. Patches jumped up on the bed, meowing loudly as if to say, "You've got to get up, Jimmy!"

Jimmy slept on. Finally Patches climbed on top of Jimmy, kneaded Jimmy's shoulder, and meowed as loudly as he could!

Jimmy woke up, startled. So did his parents in the next room. Patches bit into Jimmy's pajamas and tried to pull him out of bed just as Mom and Dad burst into the room.

Bundling Jimmy up, Mom carried him outside with Patches trailing. Dad ran to a neighbor's house and dialed 911 on their phone. Soon firefighters arrived, their truck sirens screaming, and put out the fire.

Patches could have just left the house through his cat door when he smelled the fire. He didn't have to wake Jimmy. But he risked his own life to save his playmate.

Another time, Jimmy played with toy cars in the backyard sandbox. *Buudddnnn.* He made car sounds as he pushed the toys down the sand road. Thinking about building a highway, he didn't notice two strange dogs coming near.

PATCHES SAVES JIMMY

A scruffy black dog ran out of the woods behind Jimmy's house, while a tan dog came from the other direction. The dogs spotted each other as they came closer. And they weren't friendly.

Entering Jimmy's yard, they growled at each other.

"Ggrrrrr!" the tan dog snarled.

"Gggrrrrrr!" the black dog answered, as if to say, "*You* leave! I was here first!"

Jimmy looked up as the two dogs started fighting. Teeth bared and snapping, they tumbled together. Each one tried to sink his teeth into the other dog's throat. The fighting was fierce.

Being only four years old, Jimmy didn't understand the danger of the dogfight. The only dog he knew was Uncle Bob's Sparky, who was always friendly. So when the dogs tangled, Jimmy cried, "Stop it!"

The dogs, of course, didn't obey. Jimmy got up, brushing his hands on his jeans. Jimmy's mother glanced out the window just in time to see him walk toward the dogs to stop the fight himself.

"Oh, no!" she screamed as she ran for the back door. But she needn't have worried. Patches came flying around the corner of the house. He wouldn't let those dogs hurt his Jimmy!

At a terrible risk to himself, Patches dove into the dogfight. Jimmy stopped, his eyes wide. Shrieking and clawing, Patches took on both of the dogs, who now turned their anger on the cat. What a noisy, nasty fight it was!

Dragging a garden hose, Jimmy's mom hurried over. She drenched the fighting animals with water. The dogs fled, yipping and squealing.

Patches ran, too, but Jimmy's mom scooped him up. Mom examined Patches carefully. "There don't seem to

THE ZAPPED TADPOLE

be any major hurt places," she said. And it turned out there weren't.

So Patches saved Jimmy again. Those dogs could possibly have hurt Jimmy very badly. But not with Patches around! Patches felt a similar protective love for Jimmy that Jesus feels for each one of us. Isn't Jesus special to give us animals like Patches?

12
Animals Get Spankings Too

Boys and girls, did you ever get upset when your dad or mom punished you? Did you ever think that it didn't seem fair? Did you know that animal parents discipline their youngsters too?

It would be difficult to "ground" a squirrel or a chimpanzee, wouldn't it? And I've never seen puppies get spanked, but animals do have to correct their children.

Once I saw a mother chimpanzee smack her baby—hard. While visiting a zoo in Tennessee, I stopped at the monkey habitat to watch a mother chimp nurse her baby. Picking fleas off his back and shoulders, she cuddled her little one close. He drank her warm milk greedily.

Suddenly, she jerked back, screamed, and hit her baby *Whack!* on the bottom. He cried and cried. It seems mean of her, doesn't it? But I don't think he will bite her again. And a few seconds later, she returned to snuggling with him. You see, if he kept biting, she couldn't keep feeding him. She would be too sore. He wouldn't be able to drink her warm milk.

A friend told me of a time a polar bear in Alaska made her two cubs behave—and fast! This is his story:

I took a trip to Alaska to take some wild animal pictures. Spotting a mother polar bear and twins, I set up

THE ZAPPED TADPOLE

my camera on a hill across from them. The mother bear noticed me immediately. She somehow told her cubs to get behind her so that she stood between me and them. She kept a keen eye on me to see if I meant danger. After a while, she relaxed and lay down. The cubs nestled against Mama's back, propping their chins across her.

Soon the little ones became bored. When I did nothing threatening, Mama let them start playing. Before long, they were rolling and frolicking down the snowdrift in front of her. Their play got rougher. One of them sunk his teeth into his brother's ear. Brother shrieked in pain. Mama reacted as quickly as you could say Go! All 450 pounds of her charged down that hillside to find out what was wrong with her baby. And was she ever upset!

When the cubs saw her coming, they knew they were in serious trouble. They straightened up in a hurry. Meekly, they edged up to Mama and nuzzled her as if to say, "Ah, Mom, please don't be angry! We're just little kids!"

Mama bear accepted their apology. She knew little bears need to learn that they aren't allowed to hurt each other.

Boys and girls have to learn that they can't hurt each other, too, don't they?

Another time, a mother raccoon led her youngsters on a walk through the woods. Junior raccoon kept getting into mischief. First he turned over stones to see what he could find. Then he raced in front of Mom, getting in her way. Finally, he played chase with his sister. He made altogether too much noise. Mom had enough of all this nonsense. She growled and made other warning sounds at him. He knew when Mom meant business. And she

ANIMALS GET SPANKINGS TOO

definitely meant business!

Junior rolled over tummy-up to show Mom that she was in charge. She snapped at him, warning him with her voice. But something curious happened while she scolded him. She reached out with her right paw and ever so gently placed it on his front leg. Even while she snapped, her paw rested on him as if she said, "I have to correct you, but I want you to know I still love you." Her tender touch reassured Junior that she cared very much about him, even when he misbehaved.

What do you think happens to little raccoons that make too much noise in the woods and don't pay attention? They might become breakfast for a hungry coyote. Or they might become the right sleeve of a raccoon-fur coat. So Mom's lessons were very important and necessary.

Discipline is similar for children. Usually your mom and dad have an important reason when they correct you. You have many lessons to learn when you are young, whether you are a young person—or a young animal.

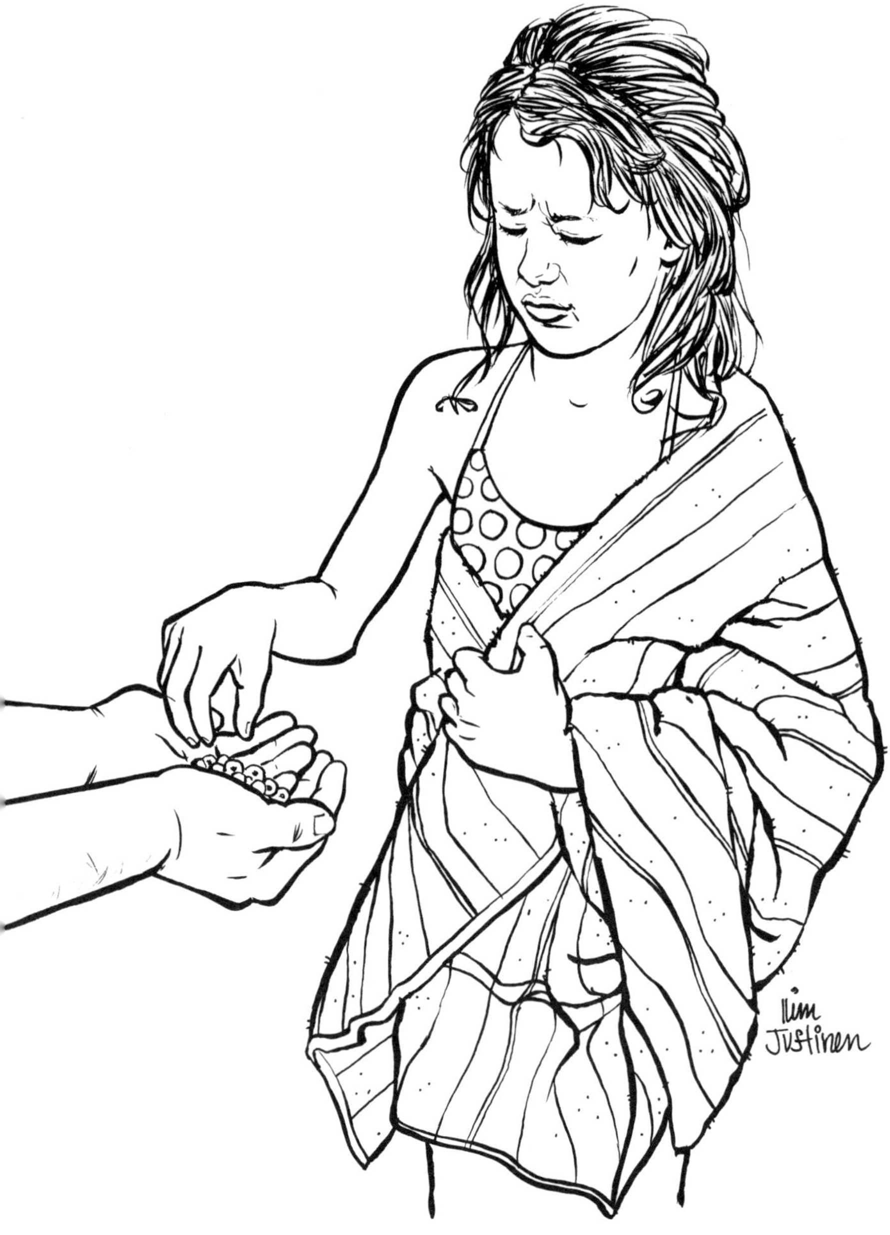
Kim
Justinen

13

The Slimy Surprise

Beth squirmed and sighed. Sitting in the front of the canoe, she felt disgusted. Usually she enjoyed canoeing with her father, but today was so-o-o-o hot, and she was tired of sitting still. She looked longingly at the cool, inviting water.

Dad had promised Beth that she could swim when they stopped for lunch. "It must be close to lunchtime now," she thought as she squinted at the scorching sun overhead.

The lake water lapped the sides of the canoe. Taking a break from paddling, Beth closed her eyes and let the motion rock her into sleepiness. She jumped as her dad said, "You look like a girl who could use a dip in the lake!"

"I sure could!" Beth agreed.

"Let's paddle over there where the road goes down into the lake." Dad pointed. "It's safer to swim where the lake bottom is smooth."

Beth didn't care as long as she got to cool off in the water. Dad's arm muscles bulged as he skillfully navigated the canoe across the lake. A sudden surprise breeze felt fabulous as it lifted Beth's short blond hair. Happiness flowed through her.

Nearing the shore, Dad pulled the dripping oars out of

THE ZAPPED TADPOLE

the lake. When the canoe drifted a couple of feet from land, Beth jumped into the water, yanked out the tie rope, and pulled the boat onto the land.

Dad grinned as his daughter hastily tied the rope around a large rock so the canoe wouldn't float away.

"You aren't in a hurry, are you?" he joked.

Beth gave a muffled answer inside her T-shirt as she jerked it over her head. In a flash, she stripped down to her bathing suit.

"May I get in now?" she pleaded.

"Sure," replied Dad.

Beth hit the water with a run and a yell. A strong swimmer, she squealed in delight at the coolness. "Ooooh," she sighed. "This feels great!"

Dad grinned as he watched Beth splash and play. Turning his back, he started to get their lunch out of the canoe. As he reached for the small cooler, his hair stood straight up as Beth screamed!

"Eeeehhhh! Eeeehhhh! Oh, help!" she screamed as she flailed and thrashed in the water. "I-I-I can't get away from it! Eeeehhh! Help!"

Dad jumped into action. Without taking the time to remove his shoes and clothes, he ran down into the lake, grabbed Beth, and carried her onto the bank. "What is it? What's wrong?" he asked, hurriedly looking over her arms and legs. "Are you hurt?" His voice trembled.

Beth answered by bursting into tears. "It felt horrible, Daddy," she sobbed. "It was cold and slimy and clammy, and it was all over my legs and stomach! I just couldn't get away from it! It was everywhere! O-o-o-hhh!" she shuddered.

"Are you OK now?" Dad asked.

"I-I think so," she stammered.

Her father held her for a minute, then cleared his

THE SLIMY SURPRISE

throat. "Will you be all right while I see if I can find out what it was?"

Beth wiped her eyes. "OK," she answered, beginning to calm down.

She watched him climb into the rear of the canoe and take out his big dip net. He lowered it into the lake until just the handle showed. He swished the net back and forth, touching nothing but water. He leaned over farther until he swished where Beth had swam. The net bumped against something solid.

"Something's here," he said.

"What is it?" Beth's voice quivered a little.

"We'll see in a minute; I'm bringing it up." Suddenly, Dad laughed. "Look what you got into, Beth!" He pulled a round, dripping, jellylike mass out of the lake.

Beth ran over to see what he held in the dip net. "Ooh, gross!" she shuddered. "What is it?"

"A cluster of bullfrog's eggs. The frogs lay their eggs in shallow water. See, each little black spot will be a tadpole." He studied the eggs.

To Beth, the eggs looked horrible. "But it's all slimy and gooey and awful!"

"I'm sure it wasn't much fun to get into, but it won't hurt you." Dad smiled.

Later, riding in the car going home, Dad reached over and patted his daughter's shoulder. "You know, Beth, I've been thinking about what happened to you today. You got quite a nasty surprise, didn't you?"

"I sure did!" Beth answered. She shivered as goose bumps rose on her skin.

"What happened to you reminds me of sin," Dad went on. "You were hot and tired, and the water looked like it would be great. But when you got into it, it wasn't nearly as pleasant as you had expected. Lots of times, sin is like

THE ZAPPED TADPOLE

that. Something that you know is wrong looks like it would be fun, but when you start doing it, it isn't nearly as exciting as you thought it would be. So you try to stop, but you find it's hard to get away from. It traps you, just like the frog eggs stuck on you."

Beth chewed her lip as she thought this over. "Do you mean like telling a lie? Like when you have to tell more lies to cover the first one? Until you are trapped in all those lies?"

Dad nodded his head. "That's exactly what I'm talking about. Of course, there's nothing wrong with swimming in the lake—that's just an example. Know what I mean?"

Beth wrinkled her nose with disgust. "Uh-huh, I think so. Maybe the next time I'm tempted to do something wrong, I'll remember how I couldn't escape from those slimy frog eggs!"

Dad chuckled. "I think I'm going to start calling you 'Frog-Eggs Beth'!"

"Da-d-dy! Don't you dare!" Beth laughed back as he tousled her hair. "Don't you dare!"

14
Selena Sunshine Madcat's Babies

Selena Sunshine Madcat was Lora, Landon, and Alicia's cat. Her fur felt warm and soft. The children giggled when they stroked her silky fur, for this always started her purring and winking. Lora, Landon, and Alicia all loved Selena Sunshine Madcat dearly.

One January day, Lora ran to her mother and said, "Mommy, Selena's getting fat." Mommy checked Selena and, sure enough, her tummy had grown big and round. "I think our Selena is going to be a mother." Mother smiled. "She has baby kittens growing inside her."

Seven-year-old Lora jumped up and down. "When will she have them? Oh, I can't wait!" she squealed. Landon, who was four, clapped his hands. "Yea, I want to see them!" he cheered. Little Alicia's eyes shone with excitement.

Mommy hugged her children. "I really don't know, but I think that she will have the kittens within a month. We all need to be very careful with her and make sure that we don't hurt her. Pet her gently, OK?"

"OK!" the kids yelled together.

Then one Sunday morning in February, Selena Sunshine Madcat came in the door and went straight to Mommy and Daddy's closet. Curious, Lora followed her.

THE ZAPPED TADPOLE

Selena found a cozy spot in the corner, turned around twice, and lay down, purring.

"Come on out, Selena," begged Lora. "Don't you want your breakfast?" Selena just kept purring. No amount of coaxing could get her out of the closet!

"Mom-my!" Lora called. "I think there's something wrong with Selena. She won't come out of the closet!"

"Maybe she wants to have her babies," Mommy said. "Let's put some old towels on the floor." So Mommy picked up Selena while Lora arranged a soft bed. When they finished, Selena stretched out and winked at them.

Lora watched for a while, but Selena didn't do anything. Soon Lora became bored and ran off to read her library book. Everyone forgot about Selena.

That afternoon, Mommy remembered the cat. Quietly, she tiptoed to the closet door and ever so gently eased it open. Guess what she saw! There lay Selena, purring happily, licking two tiny baby kittens!

"Kids, come and look!" Mommy went into the hall to call them. Lora, Landon, and Alicia scampered into the bedroom. Their shouts of "What is it?" changed into oohs and aahs as they peeked into the closet. Selena purred and purred. She was thrilled to be having kittens!

"Let's leave them alone for a little while," Mommy said. "We need to go eat our dinner. You can see her again after you eat."

After dinner, the children ran back to Mommy's closet. Do you know what they found? That's right—*three* wet little kittens! And about an hour later, Selena gave birth to one more. She made glad noises in her throat and winked at the children.

Puzzled, Landon asked Mommy, "Why is Selena so happy? She keeps purring, and we aren't even petting her!"

SELENA SUNSHINE MADCAT'S BABIES

Mommy sat down and pulled Landon onto her lap. "Selena is happy for two reasons," she told the children. "Because all of you are always gentle and kind to her, she trusts you. She knows you won't hurt her or her kittens. Usually animals want to be alone when they have their babies. It is special that Selena feels safe with you watching. She's so pleased that she purrs.

"I think she also wants to share her joy with you. God gave her the power to have little ones. He gave her great love for her kittens—just as soon as they are born. She's *full* of love and excitement!

"God taught those kittens to take their first breath and to snuggle close to their mother to find her milk too. Isn't it all wonderful?"

The children stared, thinking, as Selena washed her babies with her pink tongue. The kittens squirmed and wobbled.

"It's fantastic!" Lora whispered. "Let's thank God!"

And that's just what they did.

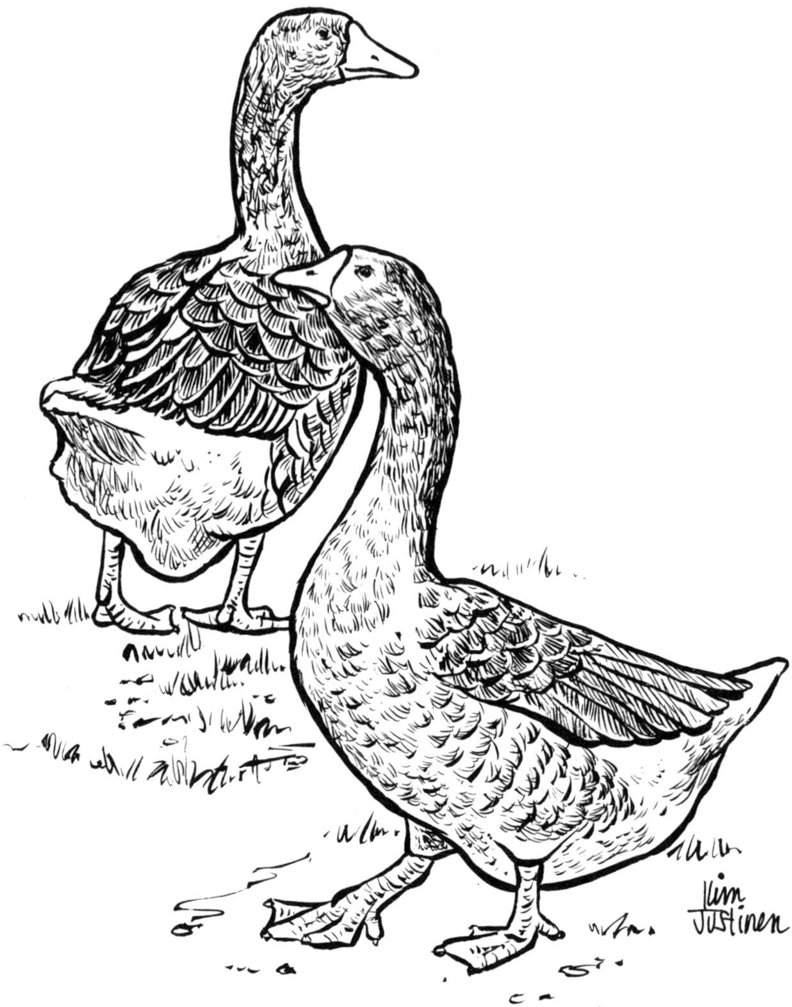
Kim Justinen

15
Galileo and Griselda

Galileo, a young, gray male goose (called a gander) honked happily. His owner, Mrs. Newman, carried something out of her car. When Galileo caught sight of gray feathers, he flapped his wings excitedly. "Yes, it *is* a wife for me!" he seemed to say.

Over the next few months, Galileo and his wife Griselda became close friends. They played, splashed in the nearby pond, and slept side by side. Whenever Mrs. Newman came out of her house with their feed, the two geese ran neck and neck to meet her. Sitting on the ground by them as they ate their grain, she taught them to eat out of her hand.

The following spring, Galileo began to pay even closer attention to Griselda. I don't think you ever saw a human father-to-be take better care of his expectant wife!

In the morning when he awakened, he prodded Griselda as if to say, "Hi, honey! Wake up; it's morning!" As she stretched, he began to preen her feathers. Ever so gently, he cleaned and smoothed out her feathers with his bill.

She turned her head this way and that so he could reach the tender spots around her eyes. Waddling

THE ZAPPED TADPOLE

around her, he evened out the dark striped feathers on the back of her head. Satisfied at last that she was perfectly groomed, he led her out of the barn for breakfast.

One sunny morning, a neighbor's dog trotted across the backyard near the two geese. Galileo instantly tore after it, beating his wings and honking. The sharp spurs on the bend of his wings drove the dog away in a hurry! And you can be sure that it didn't return.

Together, the geese built a nest just inside the barn door. Choosing only the softest feathers and straw, Galileo kept watch as he and Griselda built a home for their children-to-be. What love and protection Galileo showed for his family!

Then came the big day when Griselda started laying eggs. Galileo waggled back and forth in front of her, honking all in a tizzy. She sat relaxed and contented on her eggs, watching him. If she could have talked, I think she would have said, "Now, Galileo, calm down. You know, dear, that this will take some time before our children arrive."

Every morning after that, Galileo woke Griselda, squawking and pushing until he got her off the nest. She fussed a little at first, as if to say, "Leave me alone. I don't want to leave my eggs!" Galileo insisted on urging her toward the pond. Once she got off the nest, she seemed glad to be outside. She swam out into the water, splashing and playing. Galileo stood on the bank between her and the nest, ready to defend either.

When Galileo decided that Griselda's bath had lasted long enough, he called her. Squawking if she didn't come immediately, he seemed to say, "Come on, sweetie, it's time to go back to the nest."

As she climbed out of the water, he rushed up to groom her feathers. She spread her wings wide, flapping

GALILEO AND GRISEDLA

them to dry them. Mrs. Newman watched from her back door. "Silly Galileo!" she said with a smile, as the gander tried to help Griselda flap her wings.

Herding Griselda back to the nest, Galileo made sure that the eggs stayed toasty warm. When his mate went to graze, he guarded the eggs, making sure she wasn't gone too long. His whole life centered around overseeing his growing family.

Griselda, completely relaxed, let Galileo take over guarding the nest. She trusted him to keep her and the eggs safe. She wasn't afraid of people, and she didn't even honk when another animal came near.

What an excited, proud father Galileo was when those goslings hatched! Taking the family for a walk, Griselda led the way, while he brought up the rear, making sure that no one got left behind. He lovingly watched them eat, sometimes bringing up algae for the family from beneath the pond water.

If a storm approached, he and Griselda both drooped their wings like a lean-to, making a place for the goslings to find dry shelter. The little ones eagerly sheltered under their parents' wings.

Did you know that your heavenly Father is a lot like Galileo? He loves and protects us, just like Galileo loved his family. And our Father in heaven wants us to relax and depend on Him, like Griselda trusted Galileo. For He's even more caring than the gander. His love for us is tremendous!

16
Cisco Gets Hurt

Cisco, the black-and-white cat, knew how to have fun. Anytime his owners, Janet and Bill, wanted to play a game, Cisco was ready. He seemed to like tag best, because he often started the game himself.

Often he would hide behind the hall doorway. When Janet or Bill came near, he would bounce up and bat them on the upper leg as if to say, "Tag, you're it!" Then he would run as fast as he could before they tagged him back.

Sometimes he cheated and scurried behind the sofa, where Janet and Bill couldn't reach him. They eyed him through the crack between the sofa and the wall. There he sat with his tail swishing, grinning in his kitty way, seeming to say, "Ha, ha, you can't get me!"

Soccer was another favorite game. Bill, a college student, wrote on many sheets of paper. He often tossed Cisco a crumpled-up ball of thrown-away paper. Cisco pounced on the ball, knocking it sideways with a true soccer kick.

The cat shot across the room, getting there before the paper stopped spinning. He then "passed" the ball back across to himself. The goal was the kitchen cabinet. When he kicked the ball against the cabinet, he seemed

CISCO GETS HURT

to think that he had scored a point, because he took the ball back and started over. When Cisco grew tired of soccer, he carried the ball off in his mouth like a trophy.

Cisco loved surprises. Sometimes he would pounce on Janet and Bill to startle them. But one day, he was the one who got spooked!

Bill was eating leftover gelatin out of a big bowl. Cisco decided that this was a great time to scare him. So he crouched down and leaped—landing right in Bill's bowl of gelatin! You never saw a more surprised cat!

He quickly hopped out, shaking the gelatin off his legs with disgust. Bill laughed, trying to pet him. Cisco gave him a dirty look that said, "Leave me alone! I'm mad!" before stalking out of the room.

Sometimes Cisco had problems. He was a boy cat, and boy cats seem to think that they are owners of their own yard. If another boy cat comes into their yard, they think they have to fight over it. They often hurt each other.

One day, a big orange cat came into Cisco's yard. Cisco sank down into attack position and growled low in his throat.

"Meeowrl-l-l-l," he warned.

"Meow-r-r-r-l-l-l," answered the other cat.

Soon they tangled in a swirling, spitting, biting ball of cat fight. Janet ran out onto the front porch with a broom in her hand.

"Shoo. Get!" she yelled, swatting the cats. Getting a broom-spanking on the bottom, the orange cat took off in a flash.

Janet squatted beside Cisco.

"Are you all right?" she asked him. He felt much too ticked off to bother with her. Playing the cool cat, he marched off with his head up.

But his head became sore. Very sore. The other cat

THE ZAPPED TADPOLE

had sunk his teeth into Cisco's tender scalp, and an angry infection started there.

Janet and Bill didn't notice anything wrong for a few days. The infection, called an abscess, grew bigger.

One day, Janet came home from work and couldn't find Cisco. She called and called, but no answering meow came. She decided to look for him.

She walked around the house and checked in all the rooms. No Cisco. She scanned all his favorite sleeping spots. No Cisco. Finally, she looked in the garage. There she found Cisco, with a lump on his head the size of a tangerine.

"Oh, you poor baby!" she cried, picking him up. Feverish and hurting, Cisco lay in her arms.

Calling for Bill, she carried him into the kitchen. Bill gasped when he saw Cisco's head.

"Oh, that's awful!" he said. "It smells terrible!"

"What are we going to do?" asked Janet.

You see, Janet and Bill were a young couple just newly married. Though Janet had a job, Bill went to school, so they had to be careful about how they spent their money. They didn't have any extra money at all. They had just paid Bill's tuition, so they had no money to pay a veterinarian.

Bill poured some water into Cisco's bowl. "He feels hot. We need to get his fever down," he said.

Cisco lapped a little at the cool water. He cringed when Bill gently touched his head.

"The swelling needs to be opened so it can drain. I guess we'll have to do it," said Bill. "It can't wait until you get paid."

Janet got some peroxide and bandages while Bill dipped a small blade into alcohol to sterilize it. Soon they were ready.

CISCO GETS HURT

"Will you lance the sore while I hold Cisco?" Janet asked.

"OK," Bill said, "but be careful. Because it'll hurt, Cisco may claw and bite."

Janet lifted Cisco and laid him on the counter. Leaning over him, she grasped his legs. "Go ahead," she said.

Bill dabbed alcohol over the lump.

"E-e-e-ow!" Cisco protested.

Bill lowered his face close to Cisco's nose. "Cisco, we have to do this," he explained. "It will hurt for a minute, but it's for your own good. I'll be as fast and easy as I can be." Cisco listened as he stared at Bill.

As Bill picked up the blade, Janet whispered in Cisco's ear, "It's OK. Hold still."

"Me-e-e-ow!" he cried as Bill opened the sore spot, but he didn't scratch or squirm. He seemed to know that his master was trying to help him. He loved and trusted Bill.

Soon the abscess was draining, and Bill wrapped Cisco's head in bandages like a mummy. Still trusting his owners, the cat lay quietly and let them work. Somehow he understood the need for the bandages, too, for he didn't try to tear them off. You can be sure that Cisco got lots of loving pats and hugs afterward!

Playful Cisco quickly recovered. Within a couple of weeks, he was playing water slide on Bill's car when Bill washed it.

Did you know that Jesus wants us to be like Cisco? He wants us to trust Him as much as Cisco trusted his master. We may need to "be still" sometimes and let Him work on our problems. Just like the trusting, fun-loving cat Cisco.

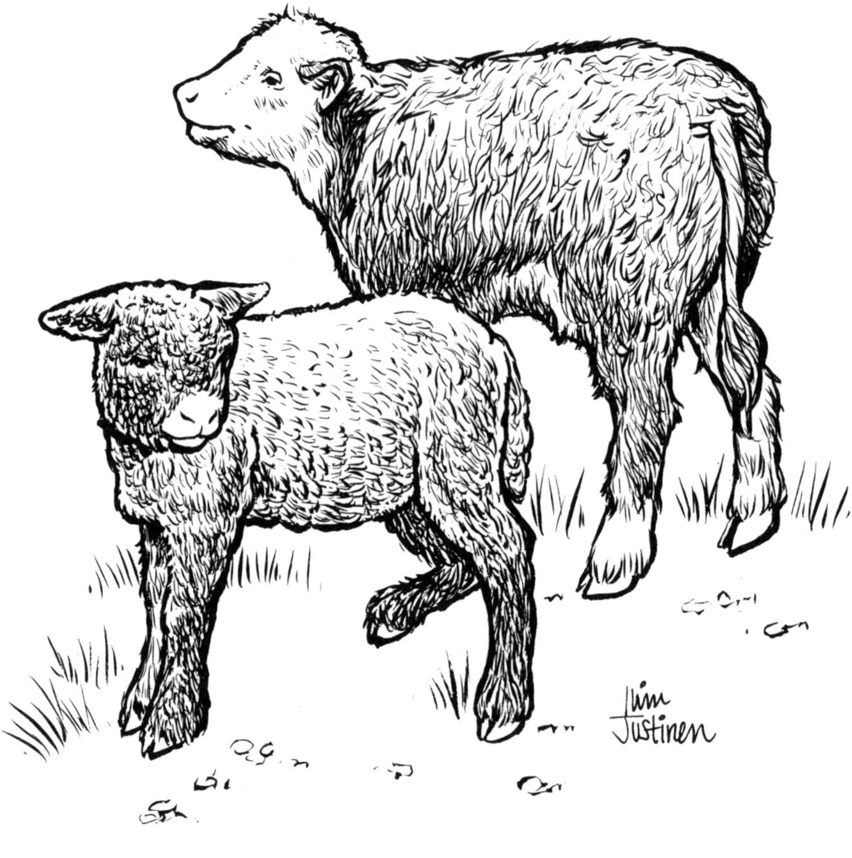
Jim Justinen

17
Little Bit and Pest

Winters are often harsh in Montana. Sometimes winter and spring seem to have a neck-and-neck race to see which one will win. If spring wins, the weather will turn warm. But if winter wins, more snow falls.

A little lamb was born on such a frosty spring morning. Winter fought to take over, and the lamb entered an icy cold world. The whirling wind whipped around the newborn baby. He wiggled wet and wobbly onto the frozen ground. Too weak to stand, he lay on the ice and snow. He tried to get up, but couldn't. He pushed all of his body up except for his right hind leg. The leg lay pressed against the ice. The leg froze to the ice.

The farmer found him that way. Clucking his tongue with a "Tsk, tsk," the farmer picked up the half-frozen lamb and carried him to the farmhouse. The mother sheep followed.

The farmer opened the preheated oven door and placed the lamb in front of it on a blanket. Soon the toasty warmth of the house thawed the baby out. All seemed fine.

But as the lamb became stronger and began to walk around, it was soon clear that all was not fine. He dragged his right hind leg. Lying on the frozen earth had

THE ZAPPED TADPOLE

permanently damaged the leg.

As the other lambs born that spring began to frolic and bounce in play, this lamb had to clumsily pull his leg around. The farmer watched while the lamb tried to keep up with the other lambs. "Look at that little bit," he would say. So the lamb became know as Little Bit.

On this farm lived a calf named Pest. The reason he was named Pest was that he was a pest. Every time the farmer or his wife went into the pasture, Pest wanted petting. He came up and rubbed against them. Pest didn't go away when the petting ended, either. "Stop it, you pest!" the farmer said. But words didn't matter to Pest. He stayed right beside them, rolling his big calf eyes. No person could be in the pasture without Pest rubbing on them the whole time!

Because Pest always wanted company and because Little Bit couldn't keep up with the other lambs, Pest and Little Bit became friends. They played their own slower games of chase-me and hide-and-seek. They often took naps together under the spreading cottonwood tree. What pals they were!

A drainage ditch snaked its way through the farm. In the late summer and fall, it held almost no water. But in the spring when the snow melted, water gushed through it. The animals soon learned to stay away from it in the spring, for an animal could be swept away faster than they could moo or baa.

No one knows how Little Bit got into the drainage ditch, but one day the farmer's wife saw a faraway white dot on the bank. She hurried to slip on a jacket. Her husband met her dashing out the door.

"What's the matter?" he asked.

"There's something in the ditch," she answered. "I think it's an animal."

LITTLE BIT AND PEST

Both of them half-ran to the ditch. It was quite a distance. They had to go up one hill and down another. But as they crossed the last hill, they had a fantastic surprise!

Little Bit was stuck in the ditch, all right. He struggled and squirmed, trying to get out, but his hooves slid in deeper with each try. It would be a hard task for any animal because the bank was steep and slippery. For a lamb with a useless leg, getting out seemed impossible. But Little Bit had a helper.

Dear old Pest was in that drainage ditch too! Head down against Little Bit's bottom, he pushed and butted his friend slowly up, up, up the hill, out of the ditch, and away from almost certain death! Little Bit and Pest climbed out just as the farmer and his wife rushed up.

When Pest bounded over for some attention that time, you can be sure he got it!

The Bible says, "Be kind to one another" (Ephesians 4:32). We can take a lesson from Pest and be kind to our friends too. We can't always save our friends' lives, but we can help each other. Let's always try to be helpful like Pest was to Little Bit.

18
A Man for a Mother

Getting tired from the long drive from Oregon to Montana, Andy Thomas rubbed his eyes. He stretched out his six-foot frame as best as he could in his pick-up truck and flipped on the radio. He grimaced as he saw another dog on the highway. "This one looks like it has just been hit by a car," he thought. But, wait, no! It didn't look like a dog!

As Andy swerved to miss whatever it was, he peered out the window. "That looks like a deer," he thought. "Yes, it *is* a deer. That's too bad." A biologist, Andy made his living by studying and working with animals. He hated to see them killed.

Pulling around the deer, he glanced in the rearview mirror. "What in the world?" he exclaimed in surprise. "Something moved. I'm sure it did!"

He braked to a stop and backed up his pickup. Forgetting about being tired, Andy bounded out of his truck and over to the deer.

"It's a deer, all right," he thought. "A doe." As he stepped closer, his mouth fell open. For he *did* see something move! Wiggling and shivering, a newborn fawn lay behind her dead mother.

Andy squatted to put his hand underneath the fawn's head. "You must have just been born," he said. "The

A MAN FOR A MOTHER

force of the car hitting your mother must have caused you to be born."

Andy sighed. What to do now? "I can't leave you here to die," he thought. He studied the fawn.

"Well, I guess you're going with me," he told the baby deer. Returning to the truck, he got an old blanket from the back. Pushing his tools to one side, he made a bed for the fawn.

Andy picked up the fawn and cradled it in his arms. The newborn animal squirmed, still shivering. Andy wrapped it in the blanket and carried it to his truck.

Finding a towel, he wiped the fawn's face. As he cleaned it, he admired the delicate white spots in the tan background of its fur. Fearless large brown eyes stared at him. Andy smiled at the deer. "You don't know that you are supposed to be afraid of me, do you? Well, you're safe with me." Watching the man, the fawn seemed to take in every word.

Andy tucked it into the blanket-bed. The fawn raised its head to watch him close the back of the truck.

Climbing back into the front seat, Andy started the motor. As he pulled away, he thought out loud, "Now what am I going to do with this baby? It seems OK, but it may be hurt. I'll take it the rest of the way home to Montana. I'll find a vet there."

Lost in his thoughts, Andy turned off the radio. The setting sun turned the scattered evergreen trees golden bright. The miles rolled by as evening approached.

Half an hour passed. Andy pushed against the steering wheel as he stretched his shoulders.

"Yiii!" he shrieked, jumping. Something had rubbed against his arm! Turning around in the semidarkness, he saw the fawn standing beside him between the two front seats.

THE ZAPPED TADPOLE

"You scared me!" he told the fawn. "What are you doing up here?" Swaying with the motion of the truck, the fawn gazed at him with its big round eyes. It wobbled as it tried to keep its balance on little sticklike legs.

As Andy turned his attention back to the road, the deer nuzzled his arm again, licking and rubbing its mouth against him.

A look of wonder crossed Andy's face as he realized what the fawn wanted. He knew all about imprinting. A newborn animal forms a love and trust for the first animal it sees—usually its mother. It looks to that animal to care for and feed it. This is imprinting.

Andy chuckled as he realized that the fawn had imprinted on him! It thought Andy was its mother. The hungry fawn wanted to nurse!

"What am I going to do with you?" he laughed quietly. "I'm not your mother."

Stopping at a convenience store, he bought some milk and warmed it in the store's microwave oven. Returning to his truck, he sorted through his belongings in the back. The fawn tottered to the back, watching his every move.

Coming up with a rubber glove, he found a nail and poked a hole in the end of one finger. He carefully poured the milk into the glove and held it out to the hungry deer.

The fawn flicked its ears as it eagerly sucked the milk. Soon the glove had to be refilled. Andy fed the fawn this way until at last it felt full and satisfied. Andy stroked its soft coat as it curled up in its bed.

Andy decided to go to the men's room before he continued his trip. He left the driver's door open a crack to give the fawn some fresh air, then walked into the restroom.

A MAN FOR A MOTHER

As he splashed cold water on his face, he heard a scratching sound. Opening the outside door, he burst into laughter. There stood the fawn! Thinking he was its mother, the fawn had followed him to the bathroom! After all, fawns in the wild follow their mothers.

Chuckling all the way, he led the deer back to the truck. They traveled the rest of the way to Montana like that—the "mother" man taking care of his little baby—the fawn.

Back home, Andy took the fawn to the veterinarian. Pronouncing the fawn healthy, the vet took it to a person who takes care of abandoned and orphaned animals. This person raised the fawn. When it grew up, it was released into the wild again—a free and happy animal whose "mother" was a man.

Who do you think taught the fawn to trust the first being it sees? You are right, God did. And He gives us *our* parents to love us and take care of us too. Let's remember to thank Him for our moms and dads.

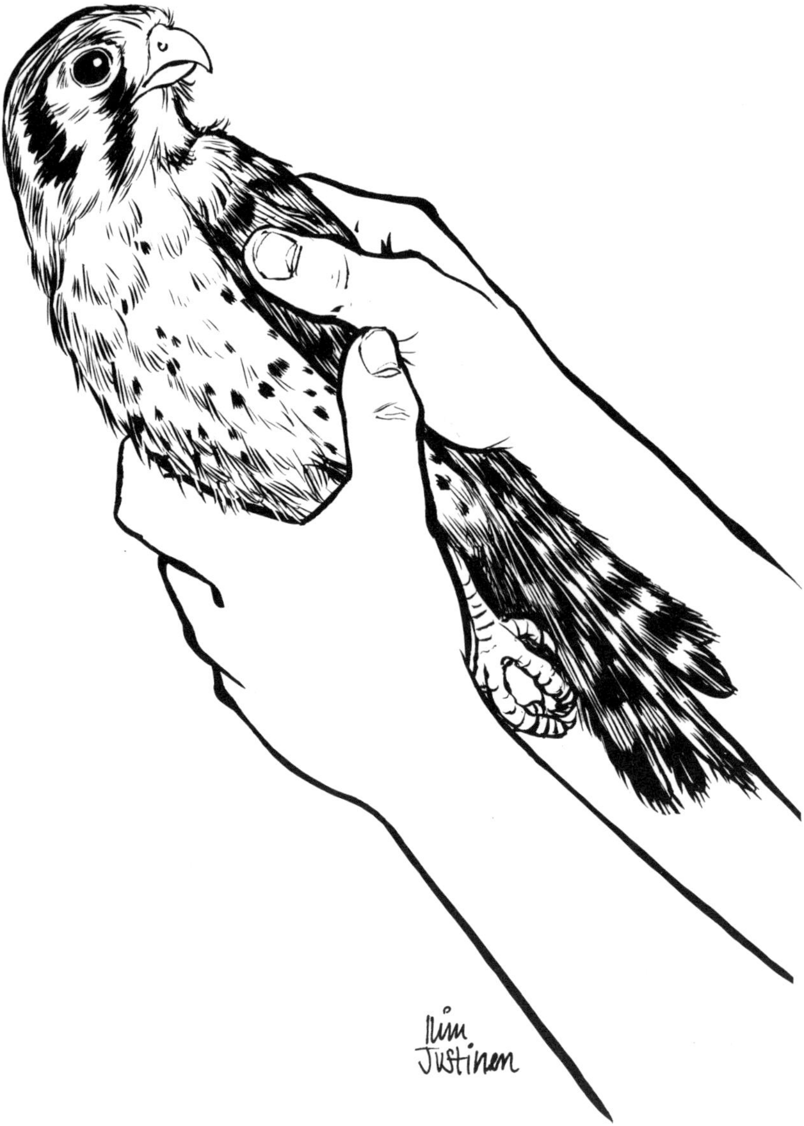
Justinen

19
Lazarus the Falcon

Dove hunting season had opened. Mr. Clarke carefully pulled a cleaning cloth through the barrel of his gun. He hummed to himself as he worked, thinking of the dove dinner he would enjoy that night. Shouldering his rifle, he went out the door. It closed behind him with a hollow, empty sound.

Later that morning, the hunter spotted a dove-sized bird hovering over a field. "Look at that bird!" he said to himself. He lifted his gun to his right shoulder. Squinting through the scope, he aimed. He squeezed the trigger. The gun exploded with a *Crack!* that echoed like a broken record.

"Got him!" Mr. Clarke shouted in triumph as he watched the bird take a swirling nosedive. He strode over to where the bird had fallen to the ground. When he came close, he realized that he had made a big mistake.

It wasn't a dove lying there, but a small falcon. "Oh, no," the man groaned. "This isn't a dove! This is a bird of prey—a falcon, I think! Boy, I'm in trouble now!" He knew that it was illegal to shoot a bird of prey. If he were found with it, he would have to pay for breaking the law.

Bright red blood shining on its wing, the falcon lay still. The hunter gazed at it for a few minutes as he

87

THE ZAPPED TADPOLE

pondered what to do. Its sharp talons and powerful beak stilled, the bird made not a flutter or sound. Finally, a little sick over shooting such a fine bird, the hunter decided to get rid of it.

Hurrying to the back of his truck, he grabbed a shovel. He tramped back to where the bird lay. Quickly, he dug a shallow hole, and, picking the bird up by the legs, plopped it into the hole. Looking around to make sure no one watched, he scooped the loose dirt over the bird.

"Well, that's done," he said as he reached into his back pocket, pulled out a handkerchief, and wiped the sweat off his forehead.

Finding his excitement over hunting gone, he tossed the shovel into his truck and started it up with a roar. He drove off without a backward glance.

Back at home, thoughts of the bird haunted him. "The falcon must have been hovering over a field mouse or some insects to catch," he sighed. "Those birds of prey are helpful—they keep down the number of rats, mice, and insects."

Unable to get the bird off his mind, he phoned his good friend, Jim Hudson.

"I trust Jim," Mr. Clarke said to himself. "Maybe he'll know something that can be done. I don't know what—the bird is already dead and buried." But the memory of the falcon made him call anyway.

"You say you shot a falcon?" Mr. Hudson asked. "Have you ever heard of the Raptor Center? They rehabilitate birds of prey—they take care of hurt hawks, eagles, and owls until they can be released into the wild again."

"But I buried it," Mr. Clarke answered. "It's dead."

"I read the other day that they can use the feathers from dead birds to help hurt ones fly again. Why don't we go dig up the bird you shot and take it in?" Mr.

LAZARUS THE FALCON

Hudson said. "You never know."

"Well, I guess so," replied Mr. Clarke. Thoughts of the once-splendid bird raced through his mind. "Maybe if I take it in, I'll feel better about it. Maybe they won't charge me a fine if I tell them it was an accident." He made up his mind. "OK. I'll meet you at your house, and we'll go to where I left the falcon."

Half an hour later, the two men dug up the bird. Mr. Clarke picked it up and gently shook off some of the dirt. Laying it on an old sheet, he carried it to the truck. As he laid the bird on the seat, Mr. Clarke gasped. The falcon moved!

"I can't believe it! It's alive!" he shouted.

His friend grinned at him. "Well, let's get it to the bird hospital," he said.

After the truck pulled up at the Raptor Center, the men carried the wrapped-up bundle inside. A young woman took the bird and disappeared through a swinging door. Mr. Clarke and Mr. Hudson sat down, waiting to find out what would happen.

A few minutes later, a tall, pleasant-faced man came out to talk with the two men. "Hello," he said as he shook their hands. "I'm Dr. White, the director of the center. What happened?"

Mr. Clarke's face turned red as he told his story. "It was an accident. I thought it was a dove," he finished.

"You probably won't be fined since you did the right thing by bringing the falcon in. It's an American kestrel, shot in the wing," Dr. White said. "It's in shock, and we'll have to do surgery on its wing. But I think we may be able to save it."

"Really? That would be great!" Mr. Clarke said.

Slowly, day by day, the bird did improve. The workers at the Raptor Center named it Lazarus, for it had been

THE ZAPPED TADPOLE

almost dead, and it had lived. Lazarus in the Bible was a man who died, and Jesus made him alive again.

In a few weeks, Lazarus started to fly in his cage, the same proud bird he had been before his accident. Then came the day when Dr. White called Mr. Clarke on the phone.

"Can you come to the Wildlife Preserve tomorrow morning at ten o'clock? We'll be doing something I think you'd be interested in. Lazarus is ready to be released."

"You bet," answered Mr. Clarke.

The next morning, Mr. Clarke squinted as he watched Lazarus quickly fly into the sunlit sky. Shading his face with his hands, he said, "You can feel God's strength and power just by watching that falcon. I'm sure that God helped raise *this* Lazarus from the dead too."

20
Withou

This story happened to me while I was writing this book. It shows the great power God has over *everything*—even cats and computers!

I was writing the story called "Sometimes Animals Get Spanked Too." Typing away on my computer, I concentrated on the polar bears and paid no attention to my cat Spencer. But he paid attention to me—he wanted a good petting, right then!

He paced back and forth around my chair, trying to get me to notice him. When I didn't, he rested on his bottom and cocked one leg up. Licking the leg clean, he peered around it to watch me.

Suddenly, he darted up onto my desk and *walked on my keyboard*! Big mistake number one. My story immediately disappeared from view. I was too stunned to move. Spencer rubbed against my hands with his soft face, unaware of the state of shock he had put me in.

In a minute I recovered enough to pick him up and put him onto my lap. He purred, closing his eyes in bliss. He had gotten what he wanted—I was finally holding him. He had no idea I really felt like screaming at him!

Frustrated, I returned to my computer. Where *was* my story? The screen asked, "Do you want to replace your

THE ZAPPED TADPOLE

story?" I thought "yes" because I had already saved part of it. Now I needed to replace it with the new parts I had just written. So I told the computer yes. Big mistake number two. *The computer totally erased my story.*

Hitting my forehead with my palm, I moaned, "Oh, no!" as I frantically tried to get the story back. I started pushing buttons like a madwoman. Spencer finally understood that something was wrong and jumped down off my lap. Perhaps he thought, "What is wrong with this crazy lady? Has she gone nuts? Well, her lap is too wobbly for me. I'm getting outta here."

I sweated and typed and gave computer commands for the next hour, all for no use. Searching through my computer manual, I tried everything I could think of to get my story back. But it was gone. Discouraged, I turned the machine off and gave up.

It was several days before I felt like writing again. I started the same story over, but I couldn't remember exactly how it had been before. The words just didn't sound right, so I decided to work on another one. Calling up the files, I found a story called "Withou."

I puzzled over "Withou." "What could this be?" I said to myself. "I've never called a story 'Withou.' " I called up "Withou," and guess what? There was "Sometimes Animals Get Spanked Too!"

Now, I never would have told the computer to call my story "Withou," and I never did. The word without didn't even appear in the entire story. I don't think I typed it when Spencer made his move. So the Lord either filed it Himself under the title "Withou," or Spencer stepped on the letters to spell "Withou" and then hit the 'file' command. I don't think that was very likely, do you? That's pretty good spelling for a cat.

The main thing I learned from this is that God is in

charge of my stories and my writing. Maybe He meant to remind me that I can do nothing without Him. And He must have had fun using my cat to teach me!

THUNDER,
the Maverick Mustang,
by Nora Ann Kuehn

Ken and his brother Bob worked hard on old man Weese's ranch to earn the black mustang. Ken loved the fiery pony with all his heart, but Thunder refused to be tamed. Ken was stubborn too. He would win the pony's affections with kindness no matter what.

Just when Thunder begins to calm down, a forest fire burns the fence posts, and he escapes. Is Ken's love strong enough to make the black mustang come home?

US$6.95/Cdn$8.70. Paper, 96 pages.

Please photocopy and complete the form below.

❏ *Thunder, the Maverick Mustang*
US$6.95/Cdn$8.70

Please add applicable sales tax and 15% (US$2.50 minimum) to cover postage and handling.

Name _____
Address _____
City _____
State _____ Zip _____

Price	$ _____	Order from your local Christian bookstore or
Postage	$ _____	ABC Mailing Service, P.O. Box 7000, Boise,
Sales Tax	$ _____	Idaho 83707. Prices subject to change without
TOTAL	$ _____	notice. Make check payable to Pacific Press.

© 1990 Pacific Press Publishing Association 2232